ULTIMATE SELF-LOVE WORKBOOK FOR TEEN GIRLS

ULTIMATE SELF-LOVE WORKBOOK FOR TEEN GIRLS

ULTIMATE SELF-LOVE

WORKBOOK FOR TEEN GIRLS

Build Confidence, Release Self-Doubt, and Embrace Who You Are

TABATHA CHANSARD, PHD

ROCKRIDGE
PRESS

For general information on our other products and services or to obtain technical support, please contact our Customer Care Department within the United States at (866) 744-2665, or outside the United States at (510) 253-0500.

Rockridge Press publishes its books in a variety of electronic and print formats. Some content that appears in print may not be available in electronic books, and vice versa.

Interior and Cover Designer: Karmen Lizzul
Art Producer: Sue Bischofberger
Editor: Elizabeth Baird
Production Editor: Ellina Litmanovich
Production Manager: Jose Olivera

Illustration © Julia Dreams via Creative Market

Paperback ISBN: 978-1-63878-601-6
eBook ISBN: 978-1-63878-396-1
R0

FOR GIGI.
FOREVER KEEP SAYING,
"I LOVE MYSELF!"

CONTENTS

INTRODUCTION

Welcome! I'm so glad you're here. My name is Tabatha Chansard, and I'm a clinical psychologist. Every day I have the pleasure of working with the most amazing and hardworking teenagers in my therapy practice. During our sessions, I hear them talk about wanting to impress their teachers, their parents, their coaches, their friends, their bosses, and even strangers on social media. I hear them worry that they're not good enough, or pretty enough, or smart enough. Your teen years are a time of rapid development. There is often immense pressure to please and appeal to others. Teens often ask me how they can feel more confident amid all this change and turmoil. To be honest, it's a question without an easy answer. But it starts by turning your attention away from others' thoughts and feelings, and toward your own. Instead of asking "How do others feel about me?" or "What can I do to make others happy?" try asking "How do I feel about myself?" or "What can I do to make myself happy?" This book is filled with exercises to help tackle these hard questions and provide some real-life answers.

If it were easy to practice self-love and build self-confidence, the world would be a much happier place and therapists like me would probably not have a job. Much like everything else we learn in life, self-love takes intention, dedication, and practice. This book will help you incorporate that practice more easily into daily life. Most teens (and adults for that matter) don't really know how or why they should even bother with self-love and self-care. They put themselves last on a long list of things that feel more important: homework, exams, chores, practice, tutoring, games, performances, friends, romantic relationships, getting a job . . . I could go on! Throughout the book, I hope to highlight what you will gain from putting yourself at the top of this list.

This book is divided into four parts. First, we will look at what self-love is and understand its challenges and benefits. Second, we will explore the six pillars of self-love: self-awareness, self-compassion, self-care, self-respect, self-trust, and self-worth. The third section uncovers how our efforts to love ourselves can positively impact our relationships. Finally, you will discover ways to integrate self-love into everyday life.

When working through this book, I encourage you to move at your own pace and find the exercises and tools that connect with you most. Not every suggestion will be right for you, and that's okay. Remember, self-love is a process. Some days it will come easily, and other days it will seem almost impossible. It takes time for the brain and body to change and grow. Even if you understand the concepts quickly, your brain and body may take much longer to adjust to them. Each day that you try is meaningful and important, even if it doesn't feel like much is changing. Be patient with yourself and the process.

I am thankful for the opportunity to help you on this journey of growth during such an important part of your life. My hope is that you will learn just how incredible you are!

"You yourself, as much as anybody in the entire universe, deserve your love and affection."

—ANON

PART 1

LET'S TALK ABOUT SELF-LOVE

"Love yourself first and everything else falls into line. You really have to love yourself to get anything done in this world."

—LUCILLE BALL

Why should you learn about self-love? As if school isn't enough, here you are being asked to learn even more! I'm sure your brain feels full as it is. But this section of the book will help you understand why self-love is vital and how it can boost other areas of your life that you care deeply about. We will begin by breaking down what self-love actually is, what it is not, and why it is important in the first place. We will also look at areas of self-love where you might already excel, then uncover areas that could use some attention.

The Basics of Self-Love

Self-love seems like a simple concept. Just love yourself, right? If only it were that easy. In reality, it can be a difficult concept to understand and an even harder thing to actually do. Every day, you are likely to say things to yourself that are mean and belittling without even noticing it. Every day, you are likely to put others first and subtly communicate to yourself that you are less important. It's time to change that. But first, we need to really understand the six main pillars of self-love:

Self-awareness: Self-awareness means having a deep understanding of your thoughts, emotions, behaviors, needs, and values. People with a high degree of self-awareness are generally able to recognize their strengths and challenges. They can evaluate themselves more realistically and are mindful of their emotions. For example, someone who is self-aware will know that they tend to procrastinate when a project due date is looming. So, they will take steps in advance to plan, organize, and work on the project ahead of time.

Self-compassion: Self-compassion involves treating yourself with the same care and understanding that you treat others. It means recognizing that you are human and will inevitably face hardship and pain. In those moments, you extend kindness and care toward yourself instead of judgment, criticism, or shame. Let's use a breakup as an example. Someone with self-compassion will acknowledge that they are feeling pain and loss and will comfort themselves with thoughts or actions that may help them through the storm. They might call on friends, snuggle with their dog, or think something like "This sucks, but I'll be okay." Someone who lacks self-compassion may be more prone to judge themselves. They have thoughts like "I was too clingy. That's why they broke up with me" or "No one will ever want to be with me."

Self-care: This is when you take action to care for your well-being, which includes your physical self, mental/emotional self, social self, and spiritual self. It can include taking a walk and drinking some water (physical self-care), journaling when you're feeling upset (mental/emotional self-care), spending time with your best friend (social self-care), and going outside and connecting to nature (spiritual self-care).

Self-respect: Someone who practices self-respect will be more prepared to set boundaries when they aren't being treated well. Self-respect is knowing how you deserve to be treated. For example, if your friend yells at you in a fight, you are expressing self-respect by saying, "I want to talk about this, but it's not okay to yell at me. Let's talk when you are feeling calmer."

Self-trust: Self-trust is having a sense of security that you will be able to meet your needs and handle difficulties that come your way. You trust in your abilities. If you have ever failed a test, you demonstrate self-trust if you are able to stay calm. You know that you can learn from the experience, study differently next time, talk to your teacher about your options, and seek outside support to learn the material if needed. You know that you will be okay because you trust in your abilities to help yourself or ask for help from others.

Self-worth: You have a good sense of self-worth when you know you are a person who is valuable and worthwhile, even with faults, challenges, and imperfections. For instance, say you excel in your English class, but no matter how hard you try, you struggle in science. Your last science exam grade was 70. With lots of studying, your next exam grade is 79. If you have a good sense of self-worth, you are likely to feel positive and proud of your improvement. Even if you didn't ace the test, you recognize that you worked hard in a subject that doesn't come easily to you.

Most of the teens I work with so badly want to feel a sense of confidence in who they are. They often seek this love and validation outside of themselves. However, what they are looking for already exists within. It's great that you are here now. You are on your way to learning how to connect with the love inside you.

> **"Self-trust means that you can take care of your needs and safety. It means you trust yourself to survive situations, and practice kindness, not perfection. It means you refuse to give up on yourself."**
>
> **—CYNTHIA WALL**

What Self-Love Is NOT

Sometimes when I start to talk to teens about self-love, I get eye-rolls and comments that self-love is selfish, conceited, or frivolous. Self-love is NOT a selfish, narcissistic act. As we work through this book, you will learn that self-love is a realistic and kind understanding of yourself. Putting yourself first tends to result in healthier relationships. It helps you be kinder and more open to the rest of the world.

Self-love also does NOT mean you have to be perfect or happy all the time. You are allowed to feel the full range of emotions and be flawed. In fact, self-love encourages it! Self-love allows you to learn and grow from mistakes and challenges. When you truly love yourself, you are aware of your imperfections. Rather than judging yourself, you take yourself as you are and grow and learn when you can.

Self-love is NOT fear, criticism, or shame. Some teens think they can criticize or bully themselves into being a better version of who they are. I've heard of teen girls looking in the mirror and criticizing every part of their body, hoping it will motivate them to change and work out more. This is not an act of self-love, and I can tell you that it never, ever works. The result is self-hatred, fear, and a sense of hopelessness. Shame, fear, and criticism always lead to negative results.

LEARNING TO LOVE

Throughout the book, you will find affirmations. These positive statements show what self-love thinking may look like. Repeating affirmations is like studying for an exam. The repetition teaches the brain that this information is important and worth holding on to. The more we repeat it, the more our brain and body absorbs the message. When you see these affirmations, close your eyes, take a deep breath, and say them aloud to yourself. Feel free to adjust the wording so that it feels like your own.

I am important. I am valuable. I matter.

Why Is Self-Love So Challenging?

I have had the joy of working with some of the most competent, bright, and compassionate teenage girls. They provide so much support and love to their friends, family, and communities. These girls are passionate about social causes and believe that others should be valued and treated with respect. They join clubs and online communities to support people who are wronged or underrepresented. Despite this outward compassion, they struggle to provide this same energy toward themselves. Why is this?

Self-love is hard for many reasons. It's hard to love yourself when you are still uncertain of who you are. Adolescence is a time of change and growth, a time when you aren't yet fully sure of yourself. It can be scary to invest energy in our evolving selves. Perhaps you've also received messages (intentionally or unintentionally) from society, your peers, or your family that you are undeserving or not good enough, that you don't really matter. Or maybe the adult women in your life also struggle with self-love (I know I do!) and haven't really modeled what it looks like.

Whatever the cause that makes self-love so challenging, I have found that teen girls tend to be fearful of asserting themselves in any way, even privately. They fear rejection and judgment and often have a sense of unworthiness. When they share their internal thoughts and beliefs about themselves, it often sounds something like this: "I don't like myself," "I'm not good enough," "What if everyone hates me?" or "I'm going to disappoint everyone." These self-deprecating thoughts get repeated over and over every day, often unconsciously. This negative thinking becomes our beliefs about ourselves. These beliefs about ourselves then impact our actions toward ourselves. Our actions toward ourselves become the way we show others how we are to be treated. A vicious cycle can take hold, and our lack of concern for ourselves can lead to pain and mistreatment.

These cycles can play out in many ways. You may have negative thoughts about your body, like "I'm ugly," "I'm fat," or "I wish I could look like her." These thoughts lead you to engage in unhealthy eating patterns, compulsively checking your body in the mirror or weighing yourself, and constantly comparing yourself to others. You may believe that you aren't good enough and that no one really likes you, thinking things like "I'm always left out" or "I'm not interesting enough." These thoughts may lead to seeking validation through relationships with others. When you do this, you may be more likely to put up with unhealthy relationships. This comes from a belief that you are undeserving of a better relationship. You get mistreated and are undervalued, and this can serve as some sort of twisted evidence or confirmation that you aren't good enough and aren't liked.

A lack of self-love can even show up as perfectionism, especially among teens. Perfectionism includes thoughts like "If I do everything perfectly, maybe no one will see how terrible I really am" or "If I get a 4.0 GPA, I'll get into a good college and *then* know I'm worthy." But it just doesn't work. How many times have you accomplished something amazing (got an A+, scored the winning goal, was voted president of a club) to still feel inadequate? This is because outside outcomes and accomplishments cannot make up for what's missing on the inside. Self-love is achieved when we value and care for ourselves regardless of the external outcomes. Because guess what—*everyone* is important and worthy of love, even when you don't get an A, have the worst game of your life, or embarrass yourself in front of your friends.

These are the cycles that I hope to help you break. This book aims to shine light on how destructive and unhelpful self-deprecation and a lack of self-love really can be. And by working through this book, I hope that you can more fully see your intrinsic value and be less scared to let yourself shine. You are important. You are valuable. You matter.

"You can't find a chance of loving yourself if you're always criticizing yourself. Self-criticism and self-love can't live in the same house."

—ANON

What Stands in YOUR Way?

It can be complicated and confusing to uncover the obstacles that stand in the way of self-love. To make progress, you will have to begin with uncomfortable work. First, you must figure out what your internal obstacles are. That means looking inward and identifying those nasty, negative thoughts and behaviors that wreak havoc without you even noticing. Then it's important to identify what the external obstacles are. Are there relationships, activities, or other environmental factors that may need some adjusting? Everyone will have different obstacles and barriers because everyone is unique. Once you have a sense of what your specific barriers are, then you can work toward getting them out of your way!

As I said, this process can be a bit uncomfortable. It means you have to be really honest and vulnerable with yourself. You have to examine thoughts and feelings that you may try to hide or ignore because they can be painful. I ask that you take it slow and be patient with yourself. Try to remember that everyone has these types of thoughts and feelings. You are not alone. It may help to have a parent, therapist, or trusted adult available to lend support or an encouraging word through this process. This is brave and challenging work, but you are strong enough to do it!

The Obstacle Course

On the path to self-love, we first must navigate a very tricky and daunting obstacle course. Once you know the obstacles you face, you will have more power and strength to make changes.

What might be some of your INTERNAL obstacles to self-love?

Examples: *Comparing myself to others; perfectionism; putting myself down; telling myself others are thinking negative thoughts about me*

....

....

....

....

....

....

....

How do these obstacles impact your behavior or daily choices?

....

....

....

....

....

....

....

~~~~~~

What are some of your EXTERNAL obstacles to self-love?

Examples: *Finding time to dedicate to myself; having too many activities and responsibilities; friends that don't treat me with respect; social media exposure*

....

....

....

....

....

....

How do these obstacles impact your behavior or daily choices?

....

....

....

....

....

....

....

....

....

~~~~~~

Why Is Self-Love Important?

As a teenager, you may have noticed that you are often trying to figure out who you are and what is important and meaningful to you. You are likely working toward gaining space and independence from your parents or other adults in your life. Your friendships and social world are more important to you than ever before. You are thinking about the future and visualizing some version of yourself that you hope to become. This period is exciting, but it can also be daunting and full of uncertainty. While you have a vision of yourself for the future, you likely don't feel that you are that person yet. You may feel scared that you won't be able to reach those goals. One unhelpful thing teens often do is bully, shame, and criticize themselves in the hope that this will help them become successful or reach this future version of themselves. As I mentioned before, this does way more harm than good.

You, on the other hand, have the opportunity to invest in yourself during this critical time. Many women miss this opportunity in adolescence. They focus on pleasing others, taking care of others, and being self-critical. Eventually they feel lost, disconnected, confused about who they are, and completely drained. They eventually must learn self-love later in life, and it is much harder to develop at that point. By committing to learning self-love now, you will be giving yourself a head start in so many areas of life. You will be able to grow into your authentic self with more ease.

Think about plants. They need sun and water to survive. But plants grow stronger and more resilient to the elements when they are provided more care. Plants are more likely to thrive, not just survive, when they receive the right amount of water, the right ratio of sun to shade, and nutrient-rich soil, and when they are trimmed and pruned. Experiments have even shown that plants grow more heartily when they are in a positive environment with encouraging words spoken to them. We, like plants, can survive with very little attention or tending to. But we need nourishment to really thrive. Self-love is the internal nourishment we need to grow stronger and more resilient to life's challenges and to reach the goals we set for ourselves.

"So plant your own gardens and decorate your own soul, instead of waiting for someone to bring you flowers."

—JORGE LUIS BORGES

SELF-LOVE IN ACTION: *Flower Visualization*

Take a moment to just sit and absorb all this new information about self-love. Find a comfortable seat and settle into it. Take a couple of deep, slow breaths in through your nose and out through your mouth. As you read the following words, visualize these images in your mind with as much detail as you can.

Imagine yourself as your favorite plant or flower. Imagine the shape you hold and the vibrant colors of your leaves or petals. Explore the scenery around you. Are you in a park, a forest, a meadow? Feel the warmth of the sun absorbing into your leaves. Feel the wind cooling you and gently swaying you. Feel your roots as they dig deep into the cool soil. Imagine self-love is refreshing water entering your roots and traveling up to quench the thirst of your leaves or petals. Feel yourself gaining strength and self-confidence as you grow tall toward the sky and your leaves stretch outward. Take another deep breath in and out, and return to your day. Hopefully you feel a little more centered and focused to care for yourself today.

The Benefits of Self-Love

Imagine you are carrying a backpack full of bricks. Each brick represents an obstacle to self-love, like self-criticism, perfectionism, fear, doubt, shame, embarrassment, guilt, judgment, disappointment, and comparison to others. This backpack weighs you down, eats up energy, makes you feel bulky and slow, and gets in your way everywhere you go. By choosing to work on self-love, you will slowly be removing these bricks from your backpack. When we make self-love a priority in our daily lives, we are likely to experience the following benefits:

A Kinder Outlook: What if you weren't your own harshest critic? Imagine internalizing the voice of your biggest advocate. It could be a best friend, a compassionate coach, a loving parent, or even a celebrity role model who has inspired you. When the voice in your head is kind, fair, respectful, and supportive, it changes your daily perspective. You become gentler and encouraging of yourself, and you feel more confident when life hands you a challenge.

More Energy: We do not realize how much energy is consumed when we are carrying that heavy backpack of self-deprecation. It causes anxiety, fear, and sleeplessness, and it makes our bodies work incredibly hard every day. Working on self-love may seem like another thing on an already impossibly long to-do list, but it will lead to a renewal of internal energy. It will stop you from wasting precious energy and resources on the wrong things, freeing you to put your energy where it matters most.

A Positive Self-Image: At the end of the day, I think every teenage girl wants to look in the mirror and feel positive about their reflection. It is unfortunately rare. Self-love removes the hateful filter through which we see ourselves. It allows you to radiate your value, confidence, and worthiness outward. It allows you to see a more accurate and authentic reflection in the mirror.

Healthier Relationships: Insecurity and fear within ourselves almost always impacts our relationships, either with our family, friends, or romantic partners. When we feel inadequate inside, we often expect others to make us feel better. We want them to fill the void created by shame and fear, to be the solution to our emptiness. Unfortunately, no person, no matter how great they are, will ever live up to this and meet those needs. When we meet our own needs and provide ourselves with love and respect, we experience healthier and more fulfilling relationships.

Better Physical Health: Negative thinking patterns cause increased anxiety and fear. These emotions trigger a physical reaction in our bodies designed to protect us from external harm, known as the fight-or-flight response. The body then produces more stress hormones, which take their toll on our physical health. When we increase self-love, our physical body is less likely to feel like it is constantly in danger. Stress hormones are reduced, and our immune system is less strained. We are likely to experience improved digestion and better sleep. Simply put, your body will thank you!

"If you're searching for that one person that will change your life, take a look in the mirror."

–ANON

TIPS AND TRICKS: *Negative Thought Tally*

As you go through your day tomorrow, keep a tally in your phone or notebook each time you notice a negative thought about yourself. Do not judge the thought, change it, or spend much time or energy on it. Just recognize its presence, mark a tally, and continue about your day. At the end of the day, look at the number of times you may have been unkind to yourself. Assume that there are likely even more thoughts that you did not catch. Take note that your negative thoughts impact you more than you realize and are likely happening more often than you realize.

Granted Wishes

We have discussed some of the areas in our lives where self-love can create positive change. Take a moment to reflect on your daily life. Check the boxes of areas that you wish you could change or improve.

I WISH . . .

☐ I could focus more

☐ I felt more comfortable with friends

☐ I felt more rested

☐ I felt more comfortable asking for help from friends

☐ I had fewer body aches

☐ I could feel more at ease

☐ I felt more attractive

☐ I felt less irritable

☐ I had more energy

☐ I had better grades

☐ I felt more comfortable in my own skin

☐ I had better control over my emotions

☐ I was a better friend

☐ I had more free time

☐ I could rely less on my phone and social media

☐ I felt more confident asking for help from teachers

☐ I liked the way my body looks

☐ I didn't ruminate on my faults

☐ I got along better with my parents

☐ I cared less about grades

☐ I wasn't rattled by criticism

Write your own:

....

....

What do you notice about your wishes? Do you think it is possible that self-love can make a difference in these areas? How?

....

....

....

The Journey to Self-Love

You have already begun the journey to self-love! Regardless of how your path weaves or how long it takes, congratulate yourself for starting. As you work through this book, challenge yourself to be open, honest, and vulnerable. The more you can connect with your authentic self, the more likely these exercises will be effective.

Sometimes being open and vulnerable can feel uncomfortable or overwhelming. If that happens, take a deep breath. Stop for a moment. You have probably struck against a part of you that needs a healthy dose of self-love. Take a pause and be proud of yourself for digging deep to care for yourself. If you then feel ready to return to the work, great. Keep at it! If you need to step away for a day or two, that's okay, too! Again, it may help to have a friend, family member, therapist, or trusted adult in your life on standby. They can help provide support and encouragement in these trickier moments. Who would that person be for you?

Let's prepare for a few of the challenges you are likely to face along the way so that you don't get too discouraged when you encounter them. First off, it's important to know that brains are LAZY! The brain likes to take the path of least resistance. It uses shortcuts to save time and energy and to be efficient. This is great when you need to make a quick decision. However, when you work hard to change your brain by thinking about things in a new way or creating new habits, the brain tends to struggle. It may go along with these new ways of thinking and acting when you are well rested and when life is easy. But during times of high stress or difficulty, the brain is likely to take that old path of least resistance because it is familiar and easy. It stinks, but it's normal when this happens. Try to be patient and intentional in encouraging your brain and body to choose the new ways of thinking. With practice and determination, the new ways will become more familiar over time. Slowly, the new pathways will become stronger, and the brain will begin to choose them over the old, now weaker pathways. Don't give up! Every time you push the brain to go a different way, you are physically altering your brain! Think about that. It's pretty cool to know that you have the power to change your brain.

The other major obstacle is time. I constantly hear how busy and overworked teens are. Your days are often long and exhausting. At the end of the day, you either crash and pass out or need time to decompress with your friends, phone, social media, YouTube, or whatever it takes to turn off your brain. So, I understand that asking you to carve out time to work in this book seems hard. However, try to remember why you picked up this book in the first place. You have goals for yourself that require some time and dedication, and you are so worth it! Remember that fostering self-love will provide you with more time, energy, and internal resources in the long run. It may make those long and stressful days seem a bit more manageable. These changes won't happen overnight, but spending time each day on this will add up. Feel free to skip around the book and do what you can, even if it is just one minute to read a quote. You deserve this time each day!

> ## "To love oneself is the beginning of a lifelong romance."
>
> **—OSCAR WILDE**

Getting Started

Practicing self-love doesn't have to be boring. You can make this time feel special and rewarding. Here are some tips on how you can add some joy into the process:

Find the time: Decide how much time you can commit to each day. See if you can find at least 10 minutes. Pick a time that is relatively consistent for you that you can make all your own. Maybe it's the window after homework and dinner but before your nightly time chatting with friends. Frame it in your mind as "me" time. This is your time to stop thinking about everyone else and focus on your own identity and growth. It's your time to be totally selfish and not feel bad about it!

Get creative: Pull out the art supplies. When you work in this book, you can use highlighters, colored pencils, gel pens, sticky notes, washi tape, stickers, and any other supplies you have. Feel free to express the real you and make this workbook all your own. Put your special stamp on it.

Create a serene space: Dedicate a comfortable space to working in the book. It can be simply a desk or your bed. But you may be more tempted to engage in the book if you are somewhere new. Perhaps a cozy chair. Or a pile of pillows on the floor. Think of this as a little "me" nook. You can even bring your favorite trinkets or pictures into the nook so you are surrounded with things that make you feel good.

Engage your five senses: Get your whole body and mind involved in this process. Wear your comfiest jammies or favorite sweater (touch); spray your favorite scent or use an aromatherapy diffuser (smell); drink a warm drink like tea or hot cocoa (taste); use dimmed or colorful lights (sight); and play some chill music or some nature sounds (hearing). Not only will this feel good to your body, but you will be pairing purposeful acts of self-love with positive sensory experiences. Over time, the brain will link feelings of contentment and self-love with these sensations. Eventually, you will be able to help trigger positivity when you engage these same senses.

Self-Love Assessment: How's Your Self-Love Today?

Let's get a better picture of where you are starting your journey. Complete this self-assessment quiz to see where you are now and where there is room to grow. Later, we will check back in to see your progress. Rate the following statements from 0 to 5, then total up your responses at the end.

0 = never	2 = sometimes	4 = most of the time
1 = rarely	3 = frequently	5 = always

1. I believe I am good enough and valuable.

    0   1   2   3   4   5

2. It is okay for me to make mistakes and not be perfect.

    0   1   2   3   4   5

3. I can communicate what I need and want with ease.

    0   1   2   3   4   5

4. I know when I am struggling and know how to support myself in those times.

    0   1   2   3   4   5

5. I believe I am worthy and deserving of love.

    0   1   2   3   4   5

6. I accept and love my body just as it is.

    0   1   2   3   4   5

7. I know my abilities and strengths and how to use them when I face challenges.

    0   1   2   3   4   5

8. My feelings are just as important as everyone else's.

   0   1   2   3   4   5

9. I do not need romantic relationships or validation from friends to feel good about myself.

   0   1   2   3   4   5

10. I make a point to take care of myself and do nice things for myself.

   0   1   2   3   4   5

SCORE:

40–50: Self-love rock star! You have a strong ability to love yourself. Keep going strong!

30–39: You have a strong foundation of self-love. Keep learning and practicing ways to strengthen your self-love abilities.

20–29: There are days you feel good about yourself and days you struggle. The more you invest in yourself with practice and patience, the more good days you will have. Don't stop!

10–19: Loving yourself fully is a challenge. But you are capable of learning how to value yourself. You're already on your way!

0–9: You're a self-love newbie. But you are capable, important, and ready to start. You're in the right place. Let's do this!

REFLECTION:

....

....

....

....

....

....

LOVING YOURSELF

> "To fall in love with yourself is the first secret to happiness."
>
> —ROBERT MORLEY

This section of the book includes exercises, practices, affirmations, and tips that will help strengthen your ability to self-love. The focus will be on the six main elements of self-love: self-awareness, self-compassion, self-care, self-respect, self-trust, and self-worth. The exercises are designed to help you gain more awareness of yourself, challenge unhelpful mindsets, and be gentler and more authentic with yourself. As you work through these exercises, try to focus on two questions: (1) What did I learn or experience from this specific exercise? and (2) How can I take this knowledge and use it in my everyday life? You'll have an even more powerful experience when you take the knowledge gained from the exercises and put it to use in your actual world.

Finding time to work through these exercises is challenging. I know how incredibly stretched you are. But each exercise in this book is designed to take no longer than 10 minutes! If you can find even five minutes a day to just focus on yourself, then you are accomplishing something incredible. You will be sending your brain the message that you are important and worth your time every day. The hope is that these exercises will also help you develop your own creative ways to show yourself care and love throughout the day, not just in a dedicated time and space. For now, just do what you can. Feel free to skip around the book and find an exercise or a short tip/trick that you can squeeze in. When you have more time to dig deeper, aim for a longer exercise. No matter how you practice, working through this book is winning!

Becoming Self-Aware

Sometimes teens get wrapped up in what others think about them and how they are being evaluated in school, sports, extracurriculars, and at home. They get so wrapped up that they forget to ask, "Who am I?" or "What do I actually think?" This is particularly difficult in the teen years because there are so many external demands placed on you. There isn't often a lot of time or space for self-reflection. It's like everyone just expects you to have it all figured out. Well, I can tell you that you should NOT have it all figured out. Rather, this is the time for figuring it out. That means learning about yourself through mistakes, challenges, failures, triumphs, accomplishments, and self-reflection.

This section of exercises will help you reflect on yourself and what is meaningful to you. Self-awareness is a deep understanding of your emotions, thoughts, behaviors, wants, needs, and values. As a teen, you likely don't have a deep understanding of all of yourself just yet. That is absolutely okay. Taking some time in this section to connect with who you are today may help you gain insight into the person you want to become. And you may surprise yourself with what you have already figured out.

Please know that self-awareness isn't always pretty. There are parts in all of us that we don't love and don't really want to shine a light on. However, self-love involves accepting yourself as you are, warts and all. The more you understand all parts of yourself, the better you are able to learn and grow adaptively. In this section, I will ask you to spend some time reflecting on thoughts and beliefs that are negative or uncomfortable. By pulling these out and becoming more aware of these aspects of yourself, you become more powerful and capable of changing them. When you are blind to these parts of yourself, they work in the background of your brain and body, wreaking havoc on your life and relationships. Use this section to take back your power. Get to know yourself just as you are today and use that knowledge to become a more purposeful you.

Who Am I?

Let's start by just getting acquainted with yourself. I often ask the teens I work with to tell me about themselves when we first meet. This turns out to be a difficult task for most of them. I think it's rare that teens get a chance to stop and think about who they are now. Rather, they are focused on who they are going to be in the future or what others think of them. Let's check in with the you from today.

What are some of your favorite things to do?

....

....

What do you look forward to each day?

....

....

What do you dread day-to-day?

....

....

What are your strengths?

....

....

....

What are some things that challenge you?

....

....

....

~~~~~~

What are some of your favorite things in your home?

....

....

....

Whom do you most enjoy spending time with?

....

....

....

What motivates you?

....

....

....

What is your biggest insecurity?

....

....

....

What are you passionate about?

....

....

....

~~~~~~

> "Until you make the unconscious conscious, it will direct your life and you will call it fate."
>
> —CARL JUNG

SELF-LOVE IN ACTION:
Me without Judgment

Imagine you live in an alternate reality where no one judges each other. You are able to freely express yourself and not fear what others may think. You can show off your quirks, your style, your insecurities, and your passions. In return, you will be valued, and others will think you are brave and cool. If this were your world, is there anything you would show about yourself that you currently keep hidden? Maybe it's your joy of singing loud even though you are tone-deaf. Maybe you would wear your favorite pair of old frayed jeans every day. Maybe you would express an opinion in your friend group that you have been holding back. Take a moment to imagine this free and uninhibited person. Are there any parts of what you just imagined that you could release into the real world in some way (e.g., singing loudly in the car with your friends)?

LEARNING TO LOVE

I don't have to have myself all figured out.
I am enough as I am.

My Values

Our values are the things or concepts that we care most about. Often, you aren't always aware of your values, but they influence what you do and how you think about yourself and the world. Bringing your values into your awareness helps you see how they may be influencing you each day. Circle five values that are most meaningful to you.

friendship	*fame*	*happiness*
love	*responsibility*	*humor*
learning	*empathy*	*peace*
money	*family*	*justice*
success	*authenticity*	*loyalty*
curiosity	*adventure*	*spirituality*
honesty	*challenges*	*purpose*
beauty	*creativity*	*trustworthiness*
compassion	*faith*	*openness*
respect	*fun*	*popularity*
kindness	*growth*	*recognition*
community	*safety*	*freedom*

Thinking Traps

One obstacle to self-awareness and self-love is getting trapped in negative thinking patterns. Remember when I said the brain is lazy? There are common styles of thinking that everyone does because the brain finds these ways of thinking a bit easier. These thinking traps are typically unrealistic and unhelpful. While they save the brain time, they may harm your beliefs about yourself.

Following is a list of some common thinking traps. When you know what these thinking traps are, you become more aware of when you are using them. This may help you remove them one by one from your mind and uncover a more realistic awareness of yourself. Check off the thinking traps you relate to, then pay attention this week to see if you fall into any of these thinking traps. Keep a tally in your phone or notebook of each time you notice yourself using a thinking trap. When you catch yourself, be curious about how it may have warped your self-awareness.

☐ **All-or-Nothing Thinking: Seeing things only as black and white. Unable to see other explanations or scenarios.**
Example: "If I don't get an A on this test, I'm a failure." (Even though a B is not failure!)

☐ **Overgeneralizing: Using one bad experience to describe all bad experiences.**
Example: "I'm *never* going to learn this! I *always* fail math!" (Even though you are making small progress and have passed many math assignments in the past.)

☐ **Mental Filtering: Paying attention only to information that confirms what you already believe about yourself, while filtering out all information that may say otherwise.**
Example: You scored two goals in your soccer game on Friday. Your teammates complimented your efforts in practice on Monday morning. Your assistant coach said, "Keep up the good work" on Tuesday. Your head coach didn't say much about your performance. You focus on your coach's lack of response and filter out all the positive feedback. This confirms your negative belief that you aren't good enough at soccer.

- **Mind Reading/Fortune-Telling: Believing you know what others are thinking or that you can predict what will happen in the future.**
  Example: You overhear a group of girls laughing. You see one of them has made eye contact with you. You assume they are laughing at you and making fun of your outfit today. In reality, you have no idea what they are thinking.

- **Catastrophizing: Blowing things out of proportion.**
  Example: "If I don't get an A in AP Physics, it will tank my GPA, and I won't get into college, and I won't get a good job, and everyone will hate me, and I'll be alone and have a terrible life."

- **Emotional Reasoning: Assuming your feelings are accurate and that there is evidence for those feelings.**
  Example: "I feel anxious. So, I know something bad is going to happen."

- **Should/Must Statements: Using phrases like "I should do this" or "I must achieve this" that make you feel guilty and like a failure.**
  Example: "I should work out every day" or "I must get the lead part in the school musical."

- **Labeling: Calling yourself names or labeling yourself negatively.**
  Example: "I'm an idiot." "I'm lazy." "I'm so awkward."

- **Personalizing: Blaming yourself for things that may not be entirely your responsibility.**
  Example: Feeling completely responsible for an argument with your friend, even though she also said hurtful things and did not act respectfully.

LEARNING TO LOVE

Today I will be curious about myself without judgment or expectation.

Self-Belief Spiral

As you can see from the thinking traps, you may often get inaccurate and unhelpful messages about yourself every day. Some of these negative messages are of your own making, whereas some come from external sources like social media, unhealthy relationships, and bad experiences. Regardless, you can get trapped in a vicious cycle of negative beliefs. These beliefs impact the way you think, act, and feel. The effects of these thoughts, actions, and feelings inappropriately confirm the negative beliefs you have. Knowing your negative self-beliefs and how they impact your daily thoughts, behaviors, and emotions can help you take control and shift into a more accurate perception of yourself. Take a look at how this cycle may play out in a person's life. Then use an example of your own in the blank diagram. Can you see how your negative beliefs may impact you day-to-day?

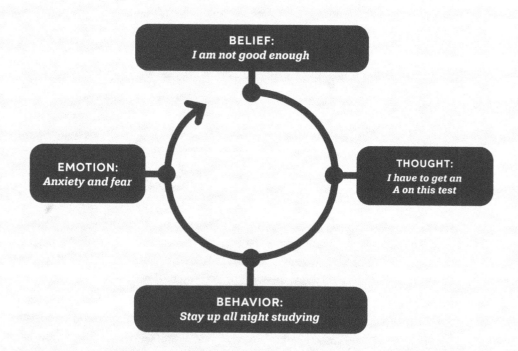

Result:

Overly tired brain struggles to learn and focus in the exam. Anxiety causes panic during the exam, making it even harder to focus. Test grade not as high. Belief that you are not good enough is reinforced.

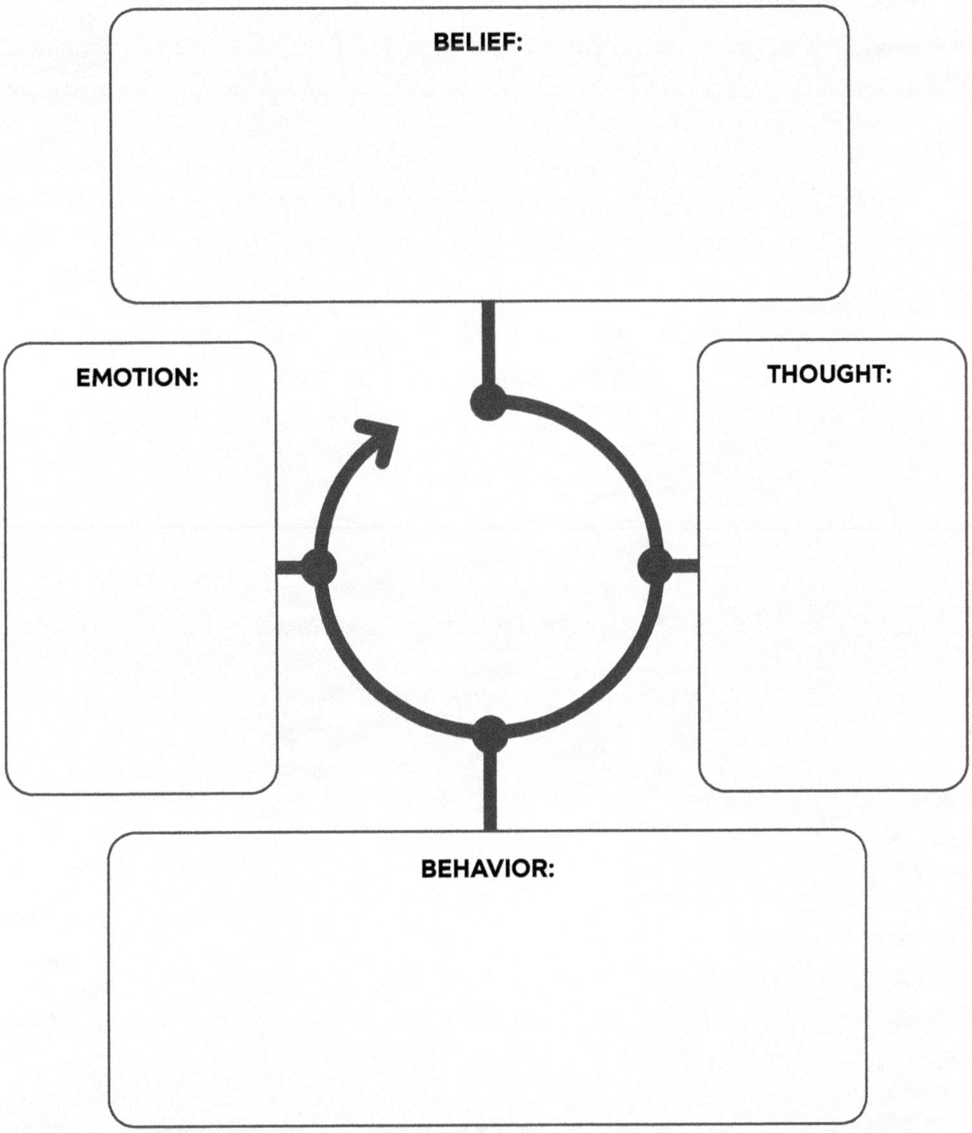

BELIEF:

EMOTION:

THOUGHT:

BEHAVIOR:

Result:

....

....

....

CONTINUED >>

Now let's see how things could be different:

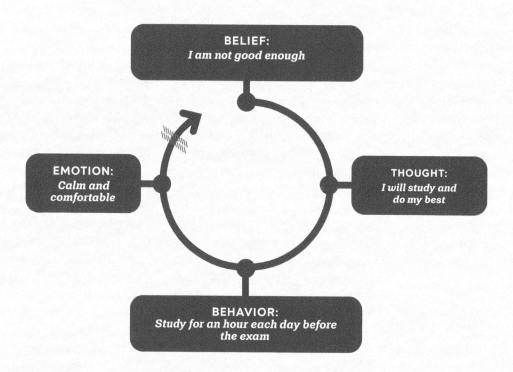

Result:

Prepared and focused, you do well on the exam. New way of thinking and behaving resulted in calmer emotions and did not reinforce an inaccurate belief.

Now see if you can think of ways to break your own negative belief spiral.

BELIEF:

EMOTION:

THOUGHT:

BEHAVIOR:

Result:

....

....

....

TIPS & TRICKS: *Check in with Yourself*

Get to know your thoughts and emotions better with an app that monitors your mood and thoughts. Apps have been specially designed to help you gain more awareness of how your thoughts and emotions may be impacting you. By logging your thoughts and feelings throughout the day, you may see patterns that you weren't aware of. This process of checking in with yourself also teaches the brain to routinely self-reflect and may help you become more attuned to yourself. Flip to the resources at the back of the book to find a list of recommended apps.

SELF-LOVE IN ACTION: *New Self-Beliefs*

As you see in the Self-Belief Spiral exercise, negative self-beliefs can hide in the background of your mind and impact your thoughts, actions, and emotions. Negative self-beliefs, under closer examination, are wildly inaccurate and generally not based in reality. Common negative self-beliefs are: "I'm not good enough," "I'm not lovable," or "I'm not worthy." Let's identify a more realistic and accurate self-belief that you can use to replace and challenge your old way of thinking and feeling about yourself. For example, "I am good enough just as I am" or "I am worthy and deserving of love." What is a more accurate self-belief for you? Write this belief on a sticky note and place it on your bathroom mirror or by your bed. Each morning, recite it to yourself. You may not fully believe it yet, but that's okay. With repetition, your brain will start to absorb it.

Conquering Challenges

Part of being you is facing a challenge, making a mistake, or failing at something. These are the times when you have probably grown the most. The problem is that teens often forget to recognize these moments and identify them as launchpads for change and growth. You mark the event away in your brain as a failure and use that experience to confirm your negative beliefs about yourself. But when you see how you have overcome challenges, you begin to see your strengths, problem-solving skills, and innate abilities that help you through difficulties. These are the parts of yourself that you need to know and connect with more often. Write about challenges you have experienced and identify what steps you took to get through these obstacles.

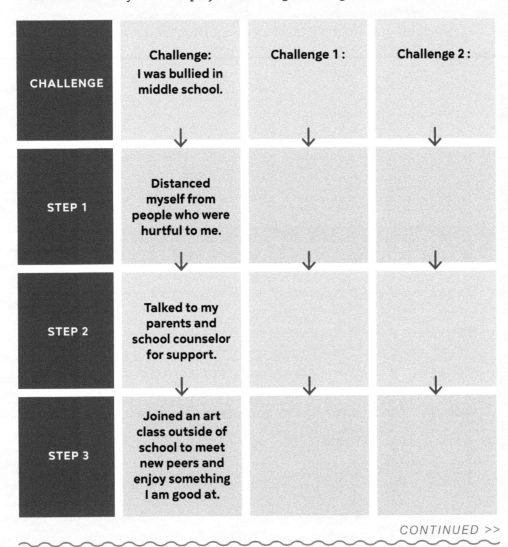

CHALLENGE	Challenge: I was bullied in middle school.	Challenge 1 :	Challenge 2 :
STEP 1	Distanced myself from people who were hurtful to me.		
STEP 2	Talked to my parents and school counselor for support.		
STEP 3	Joined an art class outside of school to meet new peers and enjoy something I am good at.		

CONTINUED >>

In the end, how did you change or grow from this experience?

Example: *I learned that I am strong and able to make new friends who treat me with respect.*

Challenge 1:

....

....

....

....

Challenge 2:

....

....

....

....

TIPS & TRICKS: *Personality Type*

Do you know your personality type? There are a couple of well-researched personality assessments that may help you learn more about yourself. These tests can help you see how your unique set of traits impacts you. By knowing your personality strengths and challenges, you may feel more empowered and less critical of yourself. Flip to the resources section at the end of the book for links to websites where you can find reliable personality assessments.

Ready Your Resources

Self-awareness is improved when you know which resources and strengths will be there to help you in tough times. What are some of your internal and external resources that help you each day?

INTERNAL RESOURCES	EXTERNAL RESOURCES
Examples: *good problem solver; able to remain calm; empathetic; creative; hardworking; organized*	**Examples:** *good friends, parents, teachers, coaches; safe home; spiritual community; sports community*

Practicing Self-Compassion

I know from working with many teen girls that they are capable of deep love and compassion. They speak of how their hearts mourn for those impacted by a variety of social issues. They scour the Internet for ways to help, for ways to be a part of the solution. Their capacity for compassion and their desire to support others is inspiring. Yet, these same teens struggle to turn that compassion inward. Applying the same kindness, openness, vulnerability, and acceptance toward themselves is much more difficult.

Self-compassion is truly connecting with the parts of yourself that are in pain, that have suffered traumas, that are scared, that are sad, that are tired and overwhelmed. Self-compassion is breaking free of the criticism, shame, and negative self-beliefs that imprison you. Self-compassion is not linked to some external outcome or achievement. Self-compassion does not care if you get an A on the exam, it does not care if you made the varsity team, it does not care if you get a date to homecoming. Self-compassion wants to hug you and nurture you in moments of difficulty. Self-compassion wants you to feel important and valuable, especially in your most challenging moments.

Without self-compassion, your negative self-beliefs will likely be much harder to shake. The internal critical voice that puts you down and bullies you is likely to be louder than your own true, authentic voice. You will likely judge yourself during your challenges and confirm your negative thoughts about yourself. These are the cycles that often keep teens trapped in anxiety and sadness and engaged in unhealthy behaviors and relationships. Now is your time to break these cycles and begin practicing self-compassion.

"If your compassion does not include yourself, it is incomplete."

—JACK KORNFIELD

Self-Compassion Quiz

As if you need another quiz in your life! This one is short, I promise! These questions will help you assess your self-compassion behaviors. Circle your responses, then tally your final score to identify your strengths and areas for improvement.

1. I treat myself with the same kindness that I treat others.

   True   **False**

2. Failure means I am not good enough.

   True   **False**

3. I stay calm and confident in myself when I make a mistake.

   True   **False**

4. When I am struggling or hurting, I know it's a part of life that all people experience.

   True   **False**

5. When something upsets me, my emotions overwhelm me and I overreact.

   True   **False**

6. I assume others are frequently thinking negatively about me.

   True   **False**

7. When I make a mistake, I obsess and fixate on what I did wrong.

   True   **False**

8. I believe all my emotions can be helpful.

   True   **False**

CONTINUED >>

9. I am not worth love or good enough as I am today.

   True   **False**

10. When I criticize myself, it helps me do better.

    True   **False**

SCORE:

Give yourself 1 point for every True response on questions 1, 3, 4, and 8. Give yourself 1 point for every False response on questions 2, 5, 6, 7, 9, and 10. Circle where your total score lies on the path of self-compassion.

0 1 2 3 4 5 6 7 8 9 10

0–3: You are on the path to self-compassion and will likely benefit from daily practice of these exercises.

4–7: Self-compassion is something you already strive to do. More practice and daily integration will help you become a self-compassionate rock star!

8–10: Self-compassion is a strength of yours! Don't stop making this a priority in your life as you grow and change!

TIPS & TRICKS: *PDA*

When you see a friend or loved one struggling, you likely show compassion through physical touch—a hug, a pat on the back, holding their hand. Touches can cause the release of chemicals in the brain that help us feel warm and fuzzy inside. You can also use physical touch to practice self-compassion. Hugging yourself may seem too cheesy and may look awkward in public. Instead, create a touch that only you will be aware is an act of self-compassion. For example, stroke your earlobe, give your shoulder a squeeze, or massage your scalp. Each day, try to give yourself a little PDA. This is a way to let yourself know that you are valuable and cared for.

LEARNING TO LOVE

I choose to learn and grow from pain and struggle.

Take Me as I Am

Part of self-compassion is accepting and appreciating who you are, with all your faults, challenges, and struggles. It's about understanding you are human and will not be perfect. It is during these times of struggle and failure that you extend yourself love and kindness, just as you would a friend or family member. In the space below, express the parts of yourself that could use your acceptance and compassion. Use words or pictures to represent your quirks, challenges, or struggles.

I accept these parts of myself.
I am worthy of love and compassion.

Time Machine Redo

Recall a time in the past, perhaps when you were a younger child, where you felt a strong negative emotion or had a very difficult experience. It is in these moments that you may establish inaccurate and hurtful beliefs about yourself, especially when you are very young and don't know better. You may have blamed yourself and criticized yourself. Then, without realizing it, you carried these emotions and beliefs about yourself into the future. This impacts your ability to self-love.

Hop into your mental time machine and talk to that younger version of yourself—even if it was just yourself from a month ago! Use the conversation bubbles to let her know that she is loved and cared for. Share with her a different way of making sense of the situation, and help her identify healthier beliefs about herself.

Example: *You were brave figuring out how to handle a situation that you had never been in before.*

CONTINUED >>

SELF-LOVE IN ACTION:
Person in Progress

Adolescence is the time of identity formation. That means you are still learning and growing. It can be hard to love yourself unconditionally if you are still discovering your identity. Take a moment to close your eyes. Inhale slowly and deeply through your nose. With your eyes closed, imagine a caterpillar turning into a butterfly. Visualize the stages of change in your mind, from a small insect crawling on the ground, to a chrysalis in metamorphosis, to a whole new form spreading colorful wings and taking flight. Much like a butterfly, you are in the process of change. Accept this process as an incredibly important part of yourself. Accept yourself as a person in progress, even in times of uncertainty. Repeat out loud: "I am a person in progress, and I love myself through change and growth."

Rotten Tomatoes

Without self-compassion, it's like there is a little movie critic in our minds constantly giving us the worst review of all time. The critic provides hurtful feedback with quips like "What a terrible performance," "You are talentless," or "Your test scores are truly horrifying." You are probably familiar with this critical voice jabbing you every day. Below, write out some of the critical reviews you often experience in your mind. Then craft a more compassionate and accurate review of yourself.

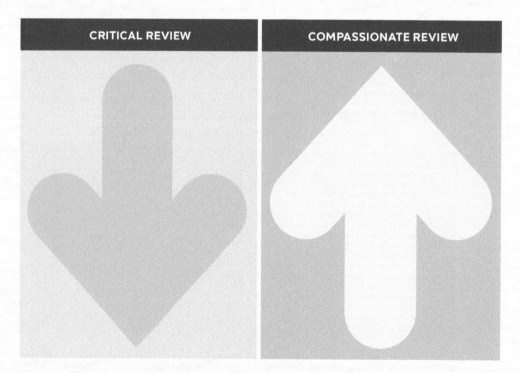

CRITICAL REVIEW	COMPASSIONATE REVIEW

TIPS & TRICKS: *Morning Mirror Mantras*

On your bathroom mirror, use a dry-erase marker or sticky notes to write quotes, mantras, or affirmations that will help you be kinder and more compassionate toward yourself. Each morning, use the mirror mantras to set an intention to be more supportive of yourself throughout the day.

Stop the Should

Sentences that have the words "should" or "must" often create a sense of inadequacy within you. "Should" statements make you feel as if you have somehow failed or weren't good enough. Reflect on times you have likely used the words "should" or "must." Then reframe the thought to be more compassionate by removing these critical words.

"SHOULD" STATEMENT	COMPASSIONATE COMEBACK
I should not have gotten a C on that test!	I studied and prepared as well as I could. I had a lot on my plate this week, and I know I juggled all the responsibilities as best I could.

CONTINUED >>

"SHOULD" STATEMENT	COMPASSIONATE COMEBACK

SELF-LOVE IN ACTION: *3 Cs*

There is a natural tendency to avoid or suppress negative emotions. But they always come back to haunt us one way or another. Rather than avoiding or judging the feeling, try the 3 Cs to practice self-compassion.

Calm: Try and create a calm space to process how you may be feeling. Close your eyes and focus on your breathing. Place your hand on your belly. Inhale through your nose very slowly. Feel your hand rise as your belly expands. Very slowly release the breath through puckered lips.

Curiosity: Invite yourself to be curious about any negative or difficult emotions you may have experienced today. Try talking to the feeling as if it is outside yourself. Ask the feeling, "What are you trying to tell me?" or "What do you need me to know?" Use curiosity to try and understand the purpose of the emotion.

Compassion: Thank your brain and body for communicating something important to you. Extend kindness and empathy to the part of yourself that was hurting or struggling. Think about how you would talk to a friend feeling this same way. Tell yourself what you would tell a friend in this moment.

The Compassionate Coach

Calming the critical voice in our mind is an essential part of increasing self-compassion. One way to do this is to internalize the voices of your most compassionate role models. Think of a coach, teacher, parent, best friend, therapist, tutor, or role model that you look up to. When your own critical voice gets too loud, focus on the voice of this person. Reflect on each situation below. How would your compassionate coach champion you through these difficult moments?

Example: I didn't get invited to homecoming.
Compassionate Coach Response: It's okay to feel disappointed, but you can make your own fun experience. You are creative and capable of finding a way to enjoy yourself. Maybe you include others who are also feeling excluded.

1. I just got dumped!

....

....

....

....

....

2. I failed my math exam.

....

....

....

....

....

3. I did not get a part in the spring musical.

....

....

....

....

4. I hate the way my body looks.

....

....

....

....

....

5. I saw on social media that all my friends hung out without me.

....

....

....

....

....

LEARNING TO LOVE

Today I will not be my own worst enemy.
Today I will be my own best friend.

Appreciating Self-Care

Imagine going a single day without your phone. Devastating and impossible, right? Your phone likely does so much for you. It connects you with your family and friends. It helps you connect with the world outside of your bubble. It organizes you. It's where you keep important memories with photos and conversations. It navigates you when you are on the road. It tells you the weather so you know how to dress. You can watch your favorite shows and listen to thousands of hours of music. It gives you access to all the information the world has to offer. The list goes on and on. This device is so important to your daily function and well-being that you always want it charged and ready to work, right? You would never let it die or not bother to charge it.

Well, your brain and body also do so much for you. Your brain is like a computer or phone. It manages a thousand different things for you every single day. It's in charge of basic functions like breathing and pumping blood. It's in charge of mental photographs and memory storage. It helps you learn new information, plan, make decisions, and regulate emotions. It controls your muscle movements and coordination. It is how you think, communicate, and see the world around you. It is the house of your belief systems and values. Your brain is your most important organ. You cannot function without it. Just like your phone, your brain needs to be charged. It is important to be thoughtful about how you protect it from crashing and burning. Unlike a phone, you can't get a new one if it is damaged or crashes.

When the brain isn't cared for and recharged daily, it begins to glitch out. In this section of exercises, you will discover steps you can take to improve your daily self-care. Learn to prioritize yourself with the maintenance of your most precious organ. When your brain is in tip-top shape, you will be better able to reach your goals of self-love.

"Don't take your health for granted. Don't take your body for granted. Do something today that communicates to your body that you desire to care for it. Tomorrow is not promised."

—JADA PINKETT SMITH

LEARNING TO LOVE

Self-care is an active way to show myself that I am important.

Maslow's Hierarchy of Needs

The concept and importance of self-care has been taught for a very long time! A psychologist named Abraham Maslow created a way to show how certain needs must first be met before you can expect to excel in other parts of your life.

Your most basic needs are at the bottom of the pyramid. In the space provided on the next page, write down obstacles you face when trying to meet these physicological needs. For example, *not enough time to sleep*, *social time keeping me up late*, *forgetting to drink water*. Then write out ways that you could strengthen your base and provide a stronger foundation for growth and self-love. For example, *prioritizing an earlier bedtime*, *setting limits on social media*, *setting alarms to drink more water*.

Self-Actualization:
seeking personal growth

Esteem Needs:
self-worth, accomplishment,
respect

Belongingness Needs:
intimate relationships, friends

Safety Needs:
security, safety

Physiological Needs:
water, food, rest

Obstacles to Meeting Physiological Needs	Ways to Improve Meeting Physiological Needs

#sleepchallenge

I know you have probably heard this before, but sleep is absolutely critical to recharging your brain and body. You are busy, and it's nearly impossible to get enough sleep with all the demands on you every day. The struggle is real. However, research shows that when teens increase their sleep, their grades improve, their SAT scores improve, their driving accidents decrease, and they are better at managing their emotions. It may seem like more sleep takes time away from studying or socializing, but it likely will help you perform better both academically and socially. Check off the tips below that you want to incorporate into your daily life that may help you get more sleep.

☐ **Adjust your daily routine. Try to sleep and wake at consistent times**

☐ **Set a firm cutoff time for work and socializing**

☐ **Create a relaxing nighttime routine and use it every day**

☐ **Limit screen use 1 hour before bed**

☐ **Improve the comfort of your space**

☐ **Use a diffuser or pillow spray with relaxing scents like lavender or eucalyptus**

☐ **Use a white noise machine**

☐ **Avoid napping**

☐ **Avoid eating or drinking caffeine 3 hours before bed**

☐ **Darken your room 45 minutes to an hour before getting in bed to let your brain know it's nighttime**

SELF-LOVE IN ACTION: *Sleep Scenes*

Do you ever lie in bed struggling to fall asleep? Do you replay your day in your head or stress about tomorrow? When the mind won't settle, giving it a task to focus on can help. Try the Alphabet Game. Once you are comfortable in bed, imagine you are at the grocery store. Imagine yourself walking through the aisles and trying to find every food item that starts with the letter A. Then look for all the food items that start with the letter B, and so on. If you notice your mind wandering, just return your mind to where you left off in the sequence. You can do this game with a variety of things as well. Mix it up with bands, TV shows, movies, first names of your classmates, cities, etc. Sweet dreams!

TIPS & TRICKS: *A Guide to Sleep*

Check out the Netflix series *Headspace Guide to Sleep*. The 20-minute episodes provide helpful information and sleep exercises you can try. It's easy to watch and can help you find ways to be the best, recharged version of yourself. Flip to the resources section for more information on this series.

Nourish to Flourish

It should be common sense that people need food to function at their best. But when life is busy, meals can come and go without notice. Nutrients are necessary to perform your most basic functions. They are especially necessary for tasks that require a lot of energy, like learning, socializing, and self-love. In the sections below, write out the changes or improvements you could make to provide your body with the nutrients it needs to be fully recharged each day.

Water **Teen girls need 78 ounces per day. How do you ensure you get enough?**

....

....

Breakfast **How do you provide your body its first dose of fuel?**

....

....

Snacks **Do you have food with you when you need it?**

....

....

Awareness **Do you know when your body is asking you to provide it with energy?**

....

....

Quality **Do you pick foods with high nutrition? How does this food help your body?**

....

....

Physical Self-Care: Mission Movement

The world is becoming increasingly sedentary. Even though you are super busy, you are also less likely to be as physically active as teens have been in the past. There is some research to suggest that reduced physical activity and increased reliance on screens is contributing to a decline in teen mental health. Increasing your movement each day can contribute to better health, both physically and emotionally. It's an opportunity to break away from the screens and to show your body some TLC. Look at these ways to increase physical movement. Check off the ones you already do (great job!) and draw a heart next to the ones you would be willing to try.

- ☐ Go for a walk
- ☐ Stretch
- ☐ Do a yoga video
- ☐ Play or practice a sport
- ☐ Lift weights
- ☐ Use an elliptical/treadmill/cycle
- ☐ Ride a bike
- ☐ Join an exercise class
- ☐ Dance (even if it's alone in your room)
- ☐ Swim
- ☐ Skateboard
- ☐ Jump rope

- ☐ Hula hoop
- ☐ Climb the stairs
- ☐ Hike
- ☐ Rock Climb
- ☐ Calisthenics (jumping jacks, push-ups, sit-ups, etc.)
- ☐ Roller skate
- ☐ Play fetch with your dog
- ☐ Garden
- ☐ Clean or do chores
- ☐ Go for a run

SELF-LOVE IN ACTION: *Screen Space*

Every summer, I speak with teens who have returned from summer camp. I ask them about their favorite part, and their responses might surprise you. I am almost always told that the break from their phones was what they really loved. They describe an increased sense of confidence and reduced anxiety as they really engaged with their peers and disconnected from social media. It makes sense. There is tons of research to support how screens and social media negatively contribute to teen mental health. Self-love is particularly damaged because you compare yourself to unrealistic images of celebrities or carefully edited pictures of your peers. Try to challenge yourself to create space from your phone. You don't need to go to summer camp to do this. Maybe it's a three-day cleanse. Maybe you give yourself one day a week with no phone or social media. However you create space away from the screen is likely going to be helpful.

LEARNING TO LOVE

My body and mind deserve my care and attention.

Spiritual Seeker

An important part of self-care is attending to your spiritual side, allowing you to connect with something bigger than yourself. This may come in many forms. Perhaps you are connected with religion. Perhaps you need some time to connect to the earth and nature. Perhaps you want to spend time exploring different forms of spirituality to find a path that works best for you. Taking time to connect spiritually has been linked to a better sense of control over emotions and improved problem-solving. Color the circles that may help you connect to your spiritual self.

My Self-Care Plan

Now that you have examined the various aspects of self-care, you can make your own self-care plan! In each section, write out your self-care goals and ideas. These acts of self-care are a way to actively send messages of self-love to your brain and body. They are small but mighty acts that will help you make important changes in your daily life.

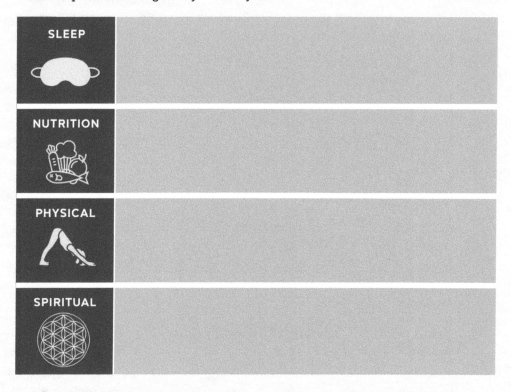

SLEEP

NUTRITION

PHYSICAL

SPIRITUAL

TIPS & TRICKS: *Small Acts of Self-Care*

Following your self-care plan may be hard on some days. When this happens, find a way to incorporate small acts of self-care into your activities. For example, when you take a shower, dim the lights, light a candle, and turn on your favorite music to make it feel more special and relaxing. When you are in the car or riding the bus, do a breathing meditation on Spotify. Get creative!

Building Self-Respect

Ask yourself this: Do you truly believe that you deserve to be treated with dignity and as if you are as valuable as everyone else? By building your self-respect, the hope is that you answer this question with a resounding YES. Self-respect is knowing without a doubt that you are important and deserve to be treated well by yourself and others. Self-respect can easily be confused with self-esteem. Society often sends confusing messages, mainly that you should value yourself based on your accomplishments or some positive outcome. You should feel good about yourself when you ace a test or score points at the game. Self-respect, on the other hand, is when you feel good about yourself just simply because you are inherently good. You feel proud of yourself when you get a C on a test because you know you worked hard and are in the process of learning something challenging. You feel accomplished even when you miss your shot because you know you aren't perfect and that you will make some and miss some.

Many teens I've worked with have been hesitant to fully embrace self-respect, believing that they will appear arrogant or conceited. It's important to understand the difference between arrogance and self-respect. Arrogance is believing that you are **better** than others. Consequently, you are likely to mistreat others, bully, or struggle to empathize with others' experiences. Self-respect, on the other hand, is knowing that you are **equally** important and valuable as everyone else. You are not better, but you certainly aren't worse. Your wants, values, needs, and desires are as important as everyone you meet. When you feel this level of self-respect, you treat yourself and others with kindness, compassion, and dignity. You are able to balance your own wants and needs while also being fair and respectful to those around you. Use the exercises in this section to get a self-respect boost!

"A girl should be two things:
who and what she wants."

—COCO CHANEL

Low Self-Respect Warning Signs

Take a look at some behaviors or thoughts that are commonly associated with low self-respect. Do you demonstrate any of these warning signs? Write your name on the top of the signs that you relate to.

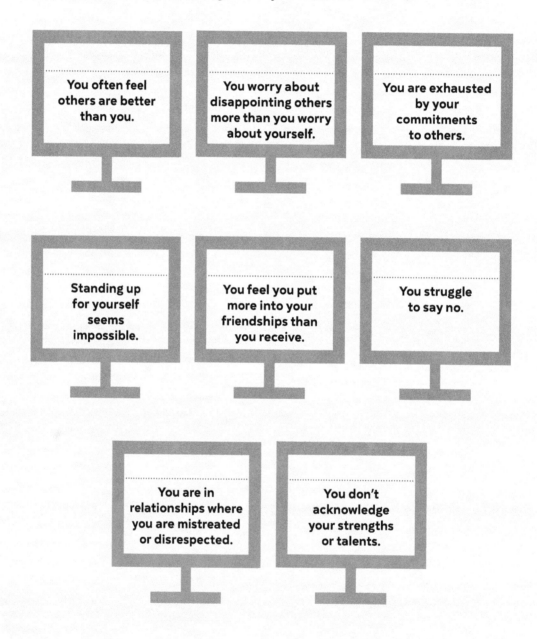

You often feel others are better than you.

You worry about disappointing others more than you worry about yourself.

You are exhausted by your commitments to others.

Standing up for yourself seems impossible.

You feel you put more into your friendships than you receive.

You struggle to say no.

You are in relationships where you are mistreated or disrespected.

You don't acknowledge your strengths or talents.

Please Stop People-Pleasing

Being thoughtful and showing others you care for them is great! However, doing things to make others love you and to feel loved yourself is called people-pleasing. This is a sign of low self-respect. People pleasers believe that if you do everything perfectly and make everyone else happy that you will be deserving of love. But here's the truth: You do not need to perform a role to be loved or respected. You are inherently lovable and valuable just as you are. When you start prioritizing your own values, others may not like that you aren't bending over backward for them anymore. And at first, that may not feel good. But you eventually realize that you have more time and space to care for yourself. Your own love from within has more space to exist. You will feel free and more in control of your life. Below are some common people-pleasing behaviors. Color in the blocks that you think you could improve upon or stop altogether.

You call people back immediately even when it's inconvenient.

You have a lot of activities that others want you to do.

You can't handle it if someone is upset or angry with you.

You fear disappointing parents, teachers, friends, etc.

You feel like you must protect people's feelings and are responsible if they're upset.

You can't turn down an invitation even if you don't really want to go.

You apologize a lot.

You frequently seek approval or permission before doing something.

You struggle to say no.

You act like you agree with everyone even if you really don't.

You avoid conflict at all costs.

You deny your own negative feelings to avoid upsetting others.

LEARNING TO LOVE

My wants and needs are equally important as everyone else's. Today I will show respect to myself.

TIPS & TRICKS: *Stop and Share*

STOP the impulse to stay quiet or hide your thoughts or feelings. Try speaking up the next opportunity you get. SHARE a thought, feeling, or opinion. This is a small way you can start building your self-respect. See how it feels.

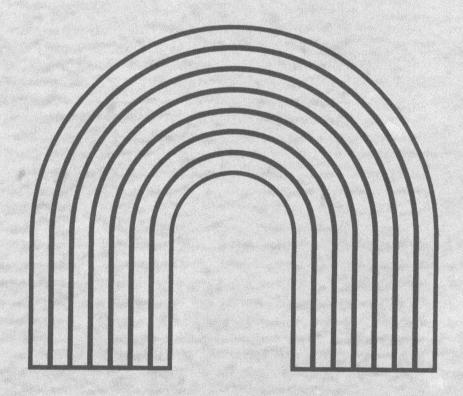

Stand Up for Yourself . . . It's Time!

I don't know about you, but sometimes when I need to stand up for myself or something I care about, my mind goes blank. I think of the best comebacks or assertions after the fact. But even after the fact can be useful. It helps you be prepared for next time. Think of a time where you needed to stand up for yourself but didn't or couldn't. What would you do differently? How would you stand up for yourself now? Write about it to practice respecting your thoughts and feelings.

WHAT I DID	WHAT I CAN DO

TIPS & TRICKS: *Keep the Compliments*

Many people who struggle with self-respect refuse to accept a compliment. They feel too uncomfortable receiving praise they don't believe they deserve. A small way to break the brain of this belief is to graciously accept the compliments. Say, "Thank you!" or "Yeah, I worked really hard on that. Thanks for noticing." It's okay to be proud of yourself and to be thankful when others also notice.

Just Say No

When you struggle with self-respect, you are likely to commit to activities that will make someone else happy, rather than doing the activity because you really value it or want to do it for yourself. When this happens, you might overextend yourself, exhaust yourself, and have little time to recharge your own batteries with activities that are meaningful to you. Practicing saying no and setting limits with your time are incredibly important skills for asserting your self-respect. It sends the message to your own brain that your wants and needs are just as important as everyone else's. Identify activities that drain you and aren't serving you. What can you let go of? What do you do that's not for you?

ACTIVITIES TO KEEP	ACTIVITIES TO TOSS

LEARNING TO LOVE

I am allowed to say no to others and yes to myself.

SELF-LOVE IN ACTION: *Visualize the No*

Visualization can help you accomplish something that may seem incredibly hard. When you visualize, you coach yourself through a scenario in your mind. This gives you more confidence about your ability to do it in real life. Try it now! Close your eyes. Imagine a real-life situation where you would like to say no. Is it a social gathering you aren't interested in? Is it giving your homework answers to your classmate? Is it gossiping behind a friend's back? Imagine yourself standing tall with your head held high. Imagine yourself asserting your boundaries clearly and succinctly. You may say something like "That's not something I am interested in doing" or "No. I don't want to." Visualize yourself saying the words that feel right to you. Visualize the most realistic outcome, not a catastrophic outcome. Imagine that the person you said no to may be annoyed, but that they accept it and move on. Imagine yourself as a powerful queen who just respected herself like a pro!

Social Media Shakedown

It's no secret that a lot of social media content is meant to influence your thinking and behaviors. Sometimes this is helpful and fun, but influencers and social media content can do great harm to your emotional health without you even realizing it. When you are struggling with self-respect, you are likely to base your feelings about yourself on comparisons to others. It may be time to clean out toxic messaging and influencers who don't model self-respect or encourage self-love in you. Answer the following questions to see how social media is helping or hurting you.

How do you typically feel when you finish spending time on social media?

....

....

Are you energized or tired after being on social media?

....

....

Do you find yourself comparing your life to those you follow on socials?

....

....

Do you compare your body to those you follow?

....

....

Do those you follow send messages of body positivity?

....

....

Do those you follow encourage you in some positive way?

....

....

Do you feel your values are accurately represented in the content you consume?

....

....

How can you adjust your feed, hide content, or follow/unfollow users to reduce your exposure to toxic or unhelpful messaging?

....

....

SELF-LOVE IN ACTION: *Today I Need . . .*

Close your eyes and slowly breath in through your nose for four seconds. Then release the air out for four seconds. Repeat this breath as you check in with each part of your body. Notice your toes, knees, and legs. Are there any sensations you feel? Notice your stomach and back. Are there tensions or pains? Notice your shoulders, neck, and arms. Are they heavy or burdened? Notice your head, mouth, nose, and eyes. Are they relaxed? As you scan your body, ask yourself, "What do you need from me today? What can I do today to show you love and respect?" Get more sleep? Go for a walk? Listen to your favorite music? Speak your mind more? Then choose one thing you can do for yourself.

Mirror, Mirror on the Wall

I'm giving you a heads-up . . . this might get awkward! Standing in front of the mirror routinely and speaking out loud your values, desires, and strengths helps build self-respect. It can rewire the part of your brain that is used to relying on others for receiving messages of respect and love. It will feel uncomfortable because you are probably not used to really seeing yourself and asserting yourself. Despite the cringe you might feel, this is an incredibly powerful way to increase self-respect and self-love. Fill in the blanks to finish the statements. Then stand in front of the mirror. Stand tall. Take up space with your body. Speak some of your completed statements:

"My strengths

are _____

_____ "

"I value _____

_____ "

"I love _____

_____about myself"

"Today I will say no to _____

_____

_____ "

Other Ideas:

▸ State your boundaries for the day.

▸ Use your "mirror mantras" to help you. Rather than just look at them, be sure to say them out loud.

▸ Say something empowering or loving to yourself.

▸ Sing an empowering song to yourself.

Developing Self-Trust

Self-doubt and insecurity are high in the teen years. You've had enough difficult times to know that the world is not all rainbows and butterflies. But you haven't had enough experience yet to know that you are more than capable of navigating life's hardships. You are still learning about your abilities, strengths, and resources. It's hard to trust at this stage of life that you are going to be okay. But you are capable of growing, learning, and excelling when things get tough.

Self-trust is when you have the knowledge that you are able to take care of yourself and manage the stressors of life. You know that you can figure it out one way or another. You know that you don't have to have all the answers, you don't have to plan too far ahead, you don't have to prepare for the worst, and you don't have to be perfect. You know that if life gives you a challenge, you can rely on your natural abilities to solve a problem, find a path, or reach out for support. By ridding yourself of negative and false beliefs about yourself, stomping out unrealistic fears, and trusting in your resources and abilities within, you will discover just how ready and able you are to face life's challenges.

> **"Don't ever doubt yourselves or waste a second of your life. It's too short and you're too special."**
>
> **—ARIANA GRANDE**

Doubtful Thinking

Think of a difficult time where you experienced a lot of self-doubt. Answer some of the following questions to explore self-doubt and how it may impact you.

Describe a situation where you experienced self-doubt.

Examples: presenting in front of your class, meeting someone new, taking a difficult test

....

....

What thoughts about yourself went through your mind?

Examples: "I'm going to mess up." "I'm going to look like an idiot." "I'm not smart enough."

....

....

Did these thoughts help you in this situation? Did these thoughts make things worse?

....

....

In the end, what did you do to get through the situation?

Examples: took deep breaths and pushed through, avoided meeting that new person, just did the best I could on the test

....

....

CONTINUED >>

If you encounter a situation like this again, how would you think differently about yourself?

Examples: "I might mess up, but no one will care, they are nervous, too." "I'm likeable and deserve to meet new people with confidence." "I studied well for this test. I know what I am doing."

....

....

TIPS & TRICKS: *DM Me*

Often when we are struggling, we seek validation or encouragement from others. It's great to use your support system to build you up. But it's perhaps even more important to be able to validate and encourage yourself. The next time you message someone for validation or support, try also sending a message to yourself. Message yourself your fears, worries, or doubts. Message yourself back as if you were replying to your best friend. You've got the answers and the confidence within. Start seeking it from yourself, too, not just from others.

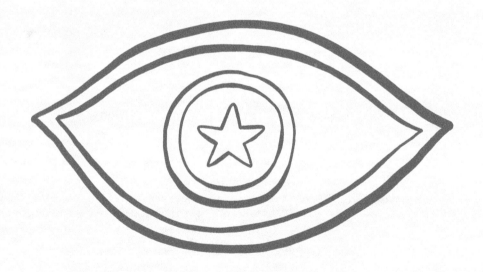

Turn Down the Volume of Self-Doubt

Thoughts of self-doubt are common. Everyone experiences them, even those who have worked hard to be confident and trusting of themselves. When self-doubt comes along, try to turn down the volume on those thoughts and increase the volume of thoughts that are more confident, accurate, and trusting of yourself.

In the low-volume boxes, write down your most common self-doubt thoughts or beliefs. For example, *I'm not good enough* or *I'll never be successful*. In the higher volume boxes, write your self-trusting thoughts or beliefs. For example, *I am capable and resourceful* or *I grow and learn from my mistakes*. As you go about your day, notice any self-doubt thoughts or beliefs. Imagine going to the volume control in your mind and actively turning down the volume on those thoughts. Then crank up the volume of your self-trust thoughts. Try to focus on the sound of those words instead.

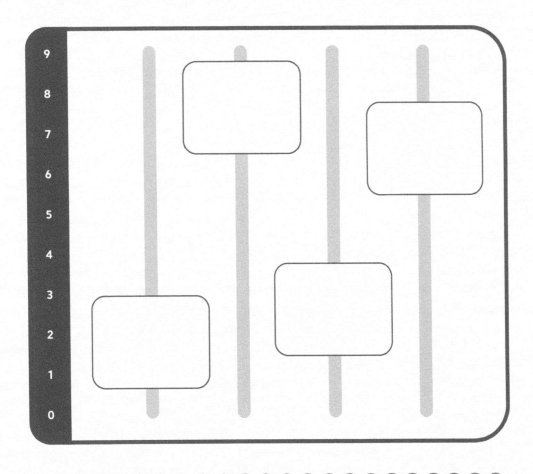

Free from Fear

Self-doubt creates fear in your mind. Fear that the worst possible outcome is likely to happen. Fear that you can't handle this challenge. Fear that you aren't good enough. Self-trust releases you from fear. When you trust in your abilities, you do not need to fear any particular outcome. You already know that you can handle the difficult emotions and that you can figure it out. Releasing yourself from fear creates more space to focus on the things that are more important to you. Answer the questions below to help free yourself from fearful thinking.

A common fearful thought I have is:

QUESTIONS TO ASK MYSELF:

Is this thought true/accurate?

Do I have evidence that the thought is true?

How likely is it that the negative outcome will actually happen?

Do I have evidence that the thought is false?

If my fear did happen, are there any solutions for dealing with it?

Am I jumping to conclusions?

If the fear did happen, will I still be okay?

Knowing myself, what outcome is most likely to happen?

SELF-LOVE IN ACTION: *Move Over, Mean Girl*

Living with self-doubt is often like being bullied by a mean girl from within. She is relentless and cruel as she puts you down and makes you question everything about yourself. You know that bullies should not be tolerated and that taking a stand is important. So why do you tolerate this mean girl behavior from yourself? Taking a stand can really feel good and empowering. So, take a moment here to get angry! Talk back! Shut down that bullying critical voice that lives inside you creating self-doubt. Let that critical voice know that she is no longer in control of you and can no longer make you feel less worthy. Imagine what you would say to this mean girl. Tell her how important you are and how you deserve to be treated with respect. Imagine yourself growing more powerful as you stand up for your true self.

SELF-LOVE IN ACTION: *Fears Floating By*

What would it be like to not be weighed down by fear and self-doubt? How much freer would you feel? Practice letting the fears and self-doubt float past you rather than sinking you. Get comfortable where you are. Close your eyes and take a few deep, slow breaths. Once you are ready, imagine yourself on a boat floating down a beautiful river. You can't control the path of the river, but you can flow with it. You can use your oars to guide you along. Imagine doubts about yourself and fears about the future floating past you. Rather than picking them up out of the river and putting them in the boat with you, you let them pass you by in the stream. You no longer need them. You are choosing to release control. Let go of the impulse to control, plan, and predict the future. Trust in yourself to navigate the waters with your strengths, skills, knowledge, and your support system. Trust in these things to keep you afloat. When self-doubt tries to sink you, return to this image of yourself capable and strong as you navigate the river of life.

LEARNING TO LOVE

I trust in myself. I am willing to see my strengths and my power.

Creative Solutions

Trusting in your ability to manage difficulties is an important part of self-love and confidence. You have likely already overcome a ton of difficult situations. Without even realizing it, you relied on your strengths, talents, knowledge, and creative problem-solving to make it through. Think of a time that you worked through a problem. In the space below, write or sketch how you dealt with this challenge. What creative solutions did you come up with? Alternatively, use the space below to think through some creative solutions to a current problem you are facing.

My Creative Solutions

LEARNING TO LOVE

I cannot control the outcome or predict the future, but I can handle it.

Bold, Brave, and Beautiful

You are already bold, brave, and beautiful even if you don't fully realize it yet. One way to release your inner strengths and abilities is to push past fears and assert yourself in ways you may have typically avoided. By trying something new or uncomfortable, you can show yourself firsthand that you are capable and that your self-doubt is unrealistic and unhelpful. In the circles below, write some brave and bold actions you can take to push back on self-doubt.

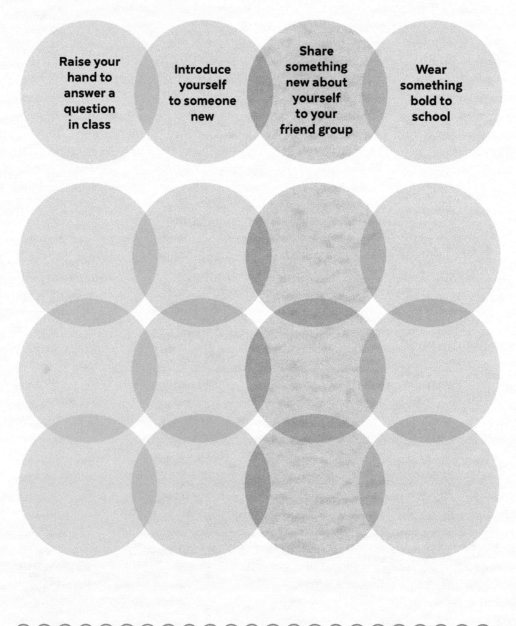

Raise your hand to answer a question in class

Introduce yourself to someone new

Share something new about yourself to your friend group

Wear something bold to school

Inner Strengths Uncovered

Most teens I have worked with really struggle to identify what their strengths are. This is typically why self-doubt is able to take hold so quickly. Knowing your strengths, talents, and skills will help you face difficulties in life. These are the tools in your toolbox that you will rely on when problems arise. Use the following questions to help uncover your inner strengths.

> **What are you good at in school or sports? What skills help you excel in these areas?**

> **What do friends or family ask for your help with?**

> **What activities do you most enjoy? What qualities about yourself draw you to those interests?**

> **What are some things that come easily to you that others may struggle with?**

CONTINUED >>

~~~~~~

> What do your friends and family admire about you? If you don't know, ask them.

> When did you overcome a challenge? What did you do or rely on to help you in that moment?

TIPS & TRICKS: *Helping Hands*

As you build trust in yourself, you will feel more self-reliant, capable, and empowered. But there is no person in the universe who can do everything by themselves. As you increase your self-trust, remember that it is also important to ask for help and support along your journey. Think about those who provide you support and can help when you are struggling. Be brave enough to ask for help as often as you need.

~~~~~~

Accepting Self-Worth

By increasing self-awareness, self-compassion, self-care, self-respect, and self-trust, you are systematically breaking the chains of self-doubt, fear, and negativity that hold you captive. With this freedom, you are now able to purposely invest energy and love into yourself. This section will help you create a strong foundation of self-worth. Without the intensity of negative thoughts and inaccurate fears weighing you down, you can start to see and trust in your value, importance, and worth.

Self-worth is a deep understanding and unshakable belief that you are valuable, lovable, and good. Having faults, making mistakes, failing to overcome challenges, and having negative feelings or experiences does not shake or break down this belief. No matter what challenges you face or how you respond to those challenges, having self-worth means you know that you are important and deserving of love and respect. With this solid belief at your core, you are better able to get through difficult times and better able to manage difficult emotions. Knowing with absolute certainty that you are worthy protects you from being taken advantage of by others and protects you from hurtful thoughts from within.

"You alone are enough. You have nothing to prove to anybody."

—MAYA ANGELOU

LEARNING TO LOVE

I release myself from unhealthy beliefs and thoughts. I choose to believe in my worth, power, and light.

Words of Worth

When life is challenging, stressful, or chaotic, our brain may take the easy path and return to old patterns of thinking. Typically, your brain will conjure up those old negative and critical beliefs. When this happens, knowing your worth can be more difficult. Practice acknowledging and communicating your worth to yourself now. It may help your brain during those more difficult moments. Below, write out a statement of your worth in each negative scenario.

Example: **Your coach benched you during an important game**	*I am a valuable member of this team, even if I don't have my best game or need to step back to let others excel*
You get a negative comment on your social media post	
Your grades are slipping, particularly in your hardest subject	
You just got dumped after dating for two months	
You are struggling to get your homework done and may have to turn in late work	

Picture This

In the Polaroids below, paste pictures, draw images, or write words that represent the real you. Think of times where you felt most like yourself. Times when you felt confident or empowered. Reflect on how you may make these snapshots more a part of your day-to-day life.

SELF-LOVE IN ACTION:
Body Image Gratitude Scan

It's an unfortunate reality that most teen girls use the mirror as a weapon of self-destruction. Today, try something different. Stand tall in front of the mirror. Close your eyes and take a deep breath. When you open your eyes, be prepared to acknowledge and thank your body for all it does for you. Start at your toes, feet, and legs. Bend your knees and wiggle your toes as you send love to them for providing you with the strength to stand. Move up to your bottom and hips. Give a little shake (it's okay to giggle!) and send thanks for providing a comfortable seat and good dance moves. Notice the core of your body. Thank your stomach and chest for providing you with the essentials of life and protecting your most vital organs. Send love and compassion up to your head and face. Give a shout-out to your eyes, nose, mouth, and ears for helping you connect to the world around you. Notice your favorite parts of yourself and how perfectly unique you are. Take one more big inhale and repeat: "I love my body and all it provides for me. I am noticing more health and beauty in my reflection."

Role Play

Reflect on the various roles that you play in your own life. Write out what values or characteristics you think make a good friend, family member, student, or other roles you play in your life (athlete, artist, sibling, etc.).

FRIEND	FAMILY MEMBER	STUDENT	OTHER ROLE

Do you feel you are worthy and important in these roles?

....

....

CONTINUED >>

Do you feel inadequate or unworthy in these roles?

....

....

Are you giving yourself enough self-love in that assessment?

....

....

How could you change your assessment to be more open to your worth?

....

....

TIPS & TRICKS: *Self-Love Symbols*

Use an object that you have with you every day to serve as a tangible symbol of your self-love, worth, and value. The object could be something like a piece of jewelry, a key chain, a crystal, a stone, or a favorite pen. When you need a self-love reminder, hold and connect with your symbol. Say one of your mantras as you use your sense of touch to bond with your symbol.

Let in the Light

What fills you with light and joy? What helps you feel whole, valued, and calm? Get creative and write, draw, collage, or use symbols to depict the things that bring out your inner light and joy. When you feel your worth is waning, remember these things or experiences to help you reconnect to yourself.

SELF-LOVE IN ACTION: *Breathe It In*

Slowly inhale through your nose as you count to four. Hold the breath in for seven counts. Slowly release the air through your lips as you count to eight. On the next breath, close your eyes and imagine the air you are breathing in is filling you up with love. It spreads through your whole being. Hold on to the love as you hold the air. With your exhale, let your insecurities leave with the breath through your mouth. Continue pulling in love, worth, respect, trust, and acceptance with your inhale. Continue releasing doubt, insecurity, and criticism with your exhales. Repeat the process until you feel a release of tension and a sense of calm take over.

Embrace Imperfection

Imperfections are a part of being human. No one is ever perfect. We strive to improve and grow, but knowing that we will never be flawless is part of what makes us normal. For today, rather than trying to fix your imperfections, take a moment to just be aware of some of them. Wear them proudly for making you unique and human. What are your perceived imperfections, flaws, or quirks that you can wear proudly without shame or guilt? Write them on the shirt below.

How might your imperfections or quirks help you or make you more endearing?

....

....

LEARNING TO LOVE

Perfection is not real. I choose to be real.
I choose to be human.

Celebrate Yourself

During your teen years, so much time is spent trying to gain more freedom and respect. As you try to grow up quickly, you likely speed past opportunities to reflect on your value and celebrate your uniqueness. Finding ways to internally celebrate yourself is a great way to boost your sense of self-worth. For example, my birthday is in October—but rather than just celebrate on the day, I internally celebrate myself the whole month. I imagine that all the pumpkins, fall decorations, Halloween candies, and fun festivities are in celebration of me! I don't share this thought with others, but I allow the month of October to fill me with joy. I allow plenty of opportunities to celebrate myself and feel the full weight of my worth. What are some ways that you could celebrate yourself? What are some quiet but special moments or experiences you could provide yourself? Describe them below.

....

....

....

....

....

....

....

TIPS & TRICKS: *Just Be a Kid*

It's easy to get caught up in the responsibilities of life and forget the simple joys from when you were younger. Take time out to just be a kid and do an activity that helped you feel amazing and gave a sense of accomplishment when you were younger. You could jump on a trampoline, swing on a swing set, play with Legos, color, craft, skip, roller-skate, or play a board game. Let loose and be a kid!

PART 3

SELF-LOVE AND RELATIONSHIPS

"About all you can do in life is be who you are. Some people will love you for you. Most will love you for what you can do for them, and some won't like you at all."

—RITA MAE BROWN

Adolescence can be one of the most difficult times to express yourself in your relationships. This is likely because your unique sense of self is still developing and your peer relationships become more important to you than any other. This is normal. But, with so much in flux and so much stock put into these relationships, you may hold back expressing yourself too much because you fear it could lead to rejection.

Rejection as a teenager is probably the scariest thing imaginable. This fear of rejection is even louder and stronger when you lack self-love. Your insecurities may lead you to get involved in unhealthy or toxic relationships, where you are devalued or taken advantage of. When you are unable to express your wants and needs in a relationship, you continue to receive the message that you are not important or worthy. Communicating your wants and needs assertively is an essential part of self-love. It's also necessary for healthy relationships with others. While asserting yourself can be intimidating, it will become more comfortable with practice. You will even find it incredibly uplifting and empowering, not nearly as likely to lead to rejection as you may think.

The skill of communicating what you want and need from others will be a lifelong superpower that will help you not only in your friendships, but also in your relationships with your family, partners, teachers, bosses, coworkers, and everyone that you encounter. In the section ahead, you will find exercises, practices, affirmations, and tips on evaluating your relationships and communicating your boundaries.

The Self-Love Six and Relationships

The previous section focused on how the six main pillars of self-love impact you directly. In this exercise, let's consider how the self-love six can impact your relationships. Under each pillar, write how you think a negative impact would affect your relationships in the top square. Then write about a positive impact in the bottom square.

Example: **Self-Awareness**

Negative Impact (without self-awareness): *I may not be firm in my values, so I go along with what others value and am too meek in my relationships.*

Positive Impact (with self-awareness): *I know what is meaningful to me, so I have better boundaries when under social pressure.*

SELF-AWARENESS	SELF-COMPASSION	SELF-CARE

SELF-RESPECT	SELF-TRUST	SELF-WORTH

LEARNING TO LOVE

I deserve to feel safe and confident in my relationships.

TIPS & TRICKS: *You're Awesome but Not Psychic*

A major hurdle to healthy relationships is mind reading. For some reason we all think we are capable of knowing what someone else is thinking about us. But the reality is that no one is psychic. When you assume you know what someone is thinking or feeling about you, what you are actually doing is projecting your own thoughts about yourself onto that person. They are YOUR thoughts about yourself. The next time you find yourself mind reading, shut it down. If you need to know what someone else is thinking or feeling, ask them! Or remind yourself that you are feeling insecure and could benefit from some self-compassion. Use a mantra to get you back on track. Try this one: "I am not psychic. But I am awesome and worthy of love."

My Relationship Zones

Most teens want to be accepted, even if they don't like the person they are seeking validation from. With self-love, you are better able to distinguish who is deserving of your energy, time, and amazing qualities. Not every person in your life deserves backstage passes and VIP access to you. You get to decide how much of yourself you share and who is an appropriate, healthy influence on you. Think about the people in your life. Who respects you for who you are? Who gives as much as they take in your relationship? Who helps you feel like your authentic self? Now place the names of these people in the zone where they belong. As you get to know people more or as relationship dynamics change, people may move in and out of different zones.

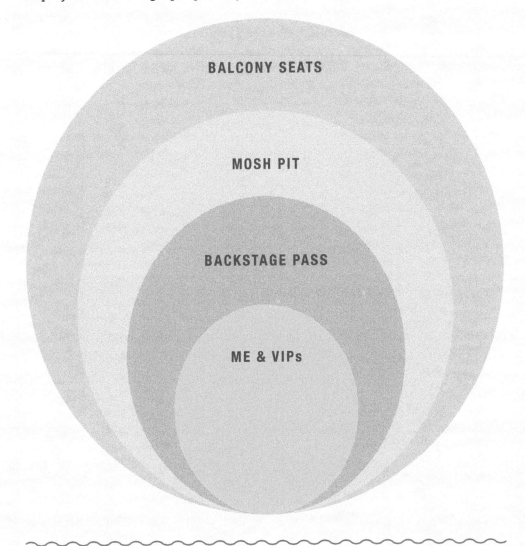

BALCONY SEATS

MOSH PIT

BACKSTAGE PASS

ME & VIPs

Rejection Recovery

Unfortunately, rejection happens a lot when you're a teenager. Relationships break up, friendships change and end, you don't make the cut when you try out for something, your teacher criticized you in front of the class, you're not invited to the party, you don't get into the college you wanted—the list goes on and on. Rejection is inevitable. The problem is that teens often use this rejection as evidence of their negative self-beliefs: "See, I'm not good enough. No one likes me, I'm worthless." You may be tempted to put up walls and block out other relationships to protect yourself from further rejection. When rejection happens, I encourage you to embrace your self-love. Use this exercise to help you work through it in a loving and realistic way.

Think of a time you recently experienced rejection.

1. *Accept and acknowledge your feelings.* Describe how you feel. Let it all out. Know that it's okay to be feeling this way.

....

....

....

....

2. *Challenge those negative self-beliefs.* What are some realistic reasons that the rejection may have happened? Maybe there is no real reason at all. Rather than immediately blaming yourself, consider the full context and explore the most realistic reasons.

....

....

....

....

3. ***Rely on self-love skills.*** How can you show yourself care, compassion, trust, and respect in this difficult moment? How would you take care of a friend dealing with rejection? Give these same acts of love to yourself.

....

....

....

....

....

....

4. ***Keep at it!*** Rejection is part of being human, and it can actually make us stronger, wiser, and more resilient. Rather than putting up walls and avoiding relationships, encourage yourself to try again. How can you get back out there? How can you learn from this experience to help you be even more successful in future relationships?

....

....

....

....

....

....

....

....

SELF-LOVE IN ACTION: *Social Shame Shift*

Teen years are full of small moments of embarrassment and social discomfort. However, toxic relationships can lead to feelings of shame, which are more intense and more difficult to shake than embarrassment. Shame arises when we believe that we are not worthy of respect and love. This can lead you to further pursue unhealthy behaviors and relationships. Practice sitting with the discomfort of shame or rejection and shifting yourself into a place of self-compassion. While holding on to something comforting (a pillow or stuffed animal), think of a time where you experienced social rejection or shame. Recall your negative thoughts and emotions. Take a deep inhale as you remind yourself that these experiences are hard and uncomfortable. As you exhale, remind yourself of your strength and that you are capable of sitting with this brief discomfort. As you inhale again, imagine that you are drawing in love and compassion for yourself. As you exhale, imagine that you are expelling these negative feelings and old toxic beliefs. Inhale your undeniable worth. Exhale the fear. Inhale your power. Exhale the control others have on you. Repeat this process until you feel released and more relaxed.

Assertiveness to the Rescue

Telling people what you want and need can be challenging. There is fear that they will think negatively about you if you speak up for yourself. Often people confuse communicating their wants and needs with "conflict" or "confrontation." These words in particular have a negative vibe. But by not communicating, you are more likely to confirm those negative thoughts about yourself, like "I'm not good enough" or "My needs don't matter." The reality is that you do matter, and asserting yourself does not need to be aggressive nor full of conflict. Check the boxes of the communication styles you use most often.

PASSIVE	ASSERTIVE	AGGRESSIVE
☐ *"Whatever you want."*	☐ *"I'm not up for that, but how about we try this?"*	☐ *"You're a loser if you don't come."*
☐ *You're not expressing your wants or needs.*	☐ *You talk and listen equally, respecting the needs of yourself and others.*	☐ *You focus only on your needs.*
☐ *You think other people's needs are more important than yours.*	☐ *You know you matter just as much as everyone else.*	☐ *You want to control others.*
☐ *You avoid problems or fear you will make problems by speaking up.*	☐ *You express yourself confidently and respectfully.*	☐ *You are bossy, rude, or manipulative.*

CONTINUED >>

Now think of a time where you wanted to assert yourself but felt uncomfortable doing so. In the lines below, write out a more assertive response where you respect your needs while remaining kind and respectful to the other person.

....

....

....

....

....

....

....

....

....

....

....

....

TIPS & TRICKS: *Sorry, Not Sorry*

When people feel insecure in themselves, it is common for them to apologize for everything. They feel not worthy and therefore feel they are a burden or nuisance in everything they do. So, nix the apologies unless there is a *real* reason. Instead of saying "I'm sorry, can I ask a question?" try something like "I have a question. Thanks!"

Conquering Awkward Conversations

All relationships come with struggles and challenges. Healthier relationships are more likely to involve communication through the difficulties. While difficult conversations with your friends or authority figures can feel awkward, they are both an act of self-love and the best approach for keeping your relationships healthy. Use the following three-pronged approach to conquer the awkwardness.

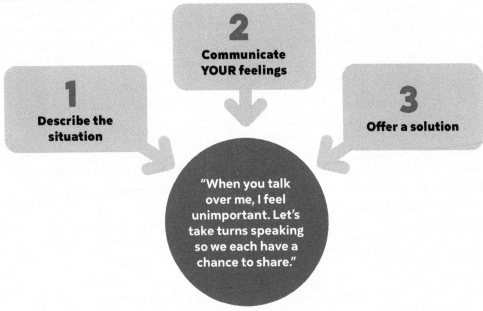

2
Communicate YOUR feelings

1
Describe the situation

3
Offer a solution

"When you talk over me, I feel unimportant. Let's take turns speaking so we each have a chance to share."

Consider a few scenarios where you have been wanting to address a concern or problem in your relationships. In the bubbles, write what you'd say using the three-pronged approach.

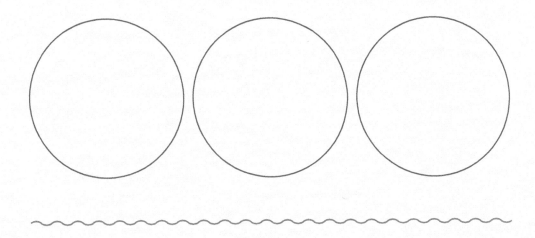

SELF-LOVE IN ACTION:
More Mirror Awkwardness

Setting boundaries and using assertive communication will take practice. A great way to do this is to try some assertive boundaries in front of the mirror. If you can do it there, it will be far easier to do it in the moment. Here are some tips for successful assertive boundaries.

1. Look confident—Stand tall and speak clearly and calmly.
2. Stay calm—Keep your emotions in check.
3. Be clear—Be specific about what you need or want.
4. Be candid—Let others know how their actions make you feel.
5. Be respectful but firm—Acknowledge their feelings and see if there is room for compromise.

Now, in front of the mirror, try some of these assertive statements on for size. Feel free to try out your own as well!

"You're standing too close. Can you please give me a bit more space?"

"You are making me feel uncomfortable. Can you please stop?"

"I need you to respect what I said or else I'll need to leave."

"I don't want to talk badly about people behind their backs. Let's change the subject."

"I know you want to go to that party, but I'm just not up for it. How about a movie or hang at my house?"

LEARNING TO LOVE

The only people who will be upset by me setting boundaries are the people who benefit from me having none. I deserve to be respected.

Boundaries Are Beautiful

Knowing your boundaries with people is such an empowering self-love skill! Boundaries are the limits and guidelines you use in your relationships. They come in many forms, including physical, mental, and emotional boundaries. Your boundaries will probably be different person to person and can change over time. Some people will require strong boundaries and limited engagement from you, like a bully. Other people will have looser boundaries in which you share more of yourself, like a parent or best friend. When you understand your own limits and how you expect to be treated, you will be better at communicating these limits to others. YOU are completely in control of your boundaries, and you can change them anytime. Use the questions below to help you identify some of your boundaries.

How do you expect to be treated in your relationships?	
What are some hard limits that you will not tolerate in a relationship?	
Can you think of times where communicating a boundary may have been helpful?	
Identify at least one boundary in the following areas: physical, emotional, and moral.	

PART 4

SELF-LOVE AND MY LIFE

"Do your thing and don't care if they like it."

—TINA FEY

So far you have completed some difficult exercises, exploring the depths of your insecurity and facing cruel self-doubts that may have held you back. You have identified the inaccuracy of those thoughts and are hopefully starting to connect with your true self. While this process has probably been challenging, you have stuck with it and are nearing the end of this book. I hope you have had impactful moments where you have seen and felt the weight of your own worth, value, and importance. Unfortunately, self-love is not something you gain and then have forever. You have to practice and make daily effort to show yourself love. This section will help you engage self-love practices in your everyday life. You will see how you can use self-love to handle specific situations and activities that many teens experience. With integration of these skills, you will be a role model for self-love and confidence. Keep going!

My Self-Love Pact

As you know, self-love requires daily practice. Making a commitment to do at least one act of self-love a day will help create new patterns in thinking and acting. Write at least one way that you can practice self-love in each of the following areas: physically, emotionally, socially, mentally, and spiritually. Make a pact with yourself to do your best to honor these goals.

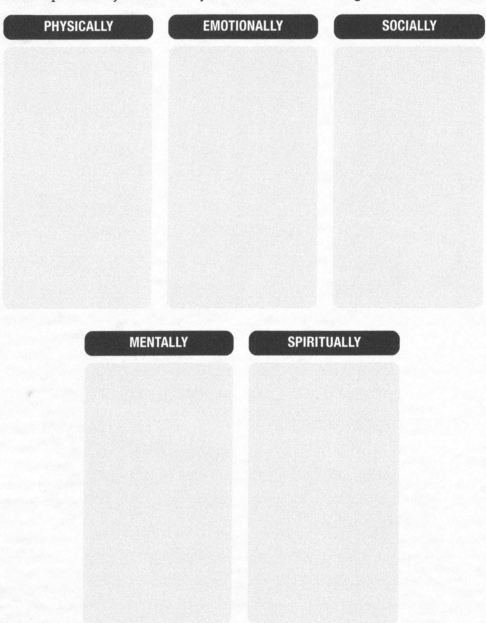

PHYSICALLY

EMOTIONALLY

SOCIALLY

MENTALLY

SPIRITUALLY

SELF-LOVE IN ACTION: *Test Day*

On days where you have a major test, game, project, or important task to complete, you are likely to feel stressed, worried, overwhelmed, distracted, and too busy for self-care. Hopefully, you have learned through this workbook that it's *especially* important to practice self-love in these times. Using your self-love skills will actually help you perform better on your important day. Try this process to help you do your best.

▸ Get to bed at a normal hour.
▸ Get up early enough so as not to be rushed in the morning.
▸ Eat breakfast and drink water.
▸ Prior to your test, game, or task pause, breathe in and out through your nose slowly.
▸ Visualize yourself approaching your task with confidence and calmness.

If your stress rises, remind yourself: "I am important and will be okay no matter the outcome of this singular experience. I am more than this one test."

LEARNING TO LOVE

I choose to release myself from negative self-talk. I choose to embrace myself with compassion, respect, and love.

#nofilter

Think back to the Self-Belief Spiral exercise on page 30. Remember how negative self-beliefs can influence our thoughts and actions? Think of these beliefs as filters on your photos. The original photo is reality, but the filter distorts the real experience. Some core beliefs are positive filters, like adding hearts and sparkles to your image. But negative core beliefs distort in unhelpful and hurtful ways, like turning your face into a creepy monster. The next time you are having a difficult experience, challenge yourself to change the filter. Can you look at the experience through a self-love filter versus a filter of fear and insecurity? For this exercise, think about a difficult experience you may be having. On the Negative Filter phone, write or draw how this filter may be distorting your experience. On the No Filter phone, write or draw what the experience might look like when you remove your negative self-beliefs and see the situation with a bit more clarity and reality.

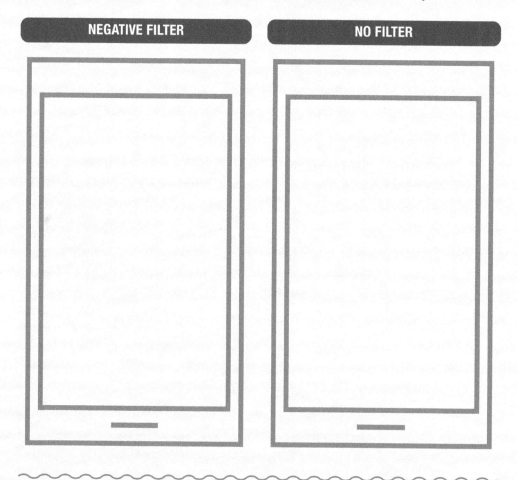

| NEGATIVE FILTER | NO FILTER |

Getting Out of My Comfort Zone

Feeling more confident yet? As your self-love continues to expand, you may feel lighter and more at ease in situations that previously felt awkward or uncomfortable. You can embrace this newfound confidence by stepping outside your comfort zones to discover new strengths and skills. In the space below, think of some things you have wanted to do or say. Put them in the zones according to how comfortable you'd be trying them. As your self-love and confidence grow, see if you can work your way to the outer zones.

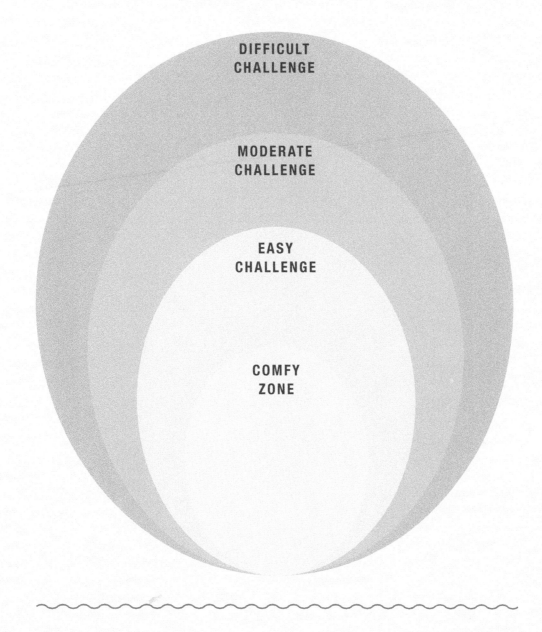

DIFFICULT
CHALLENGE

MODERATE
CHALLENGE

EASY
CHALLENGE

COMFY
ZONE

TIPS & TRICKS: *Accomplishment Check*

Pause to acknowledge something you have accomplished recently. Negative self-beliefs tend to cause people to ignore their accomplishments, big and small. They focus only on events and experiences that bring them down. Push back on those negative self-beliefs and give yourself some props. It can be as small as "I got up on time today!" or "I held the door open for someone." Or as large as "I scored the winning goal in soccer!" or "I got the lead in the play!" Either way, get into a habit of recognizing yourself and your efforts!

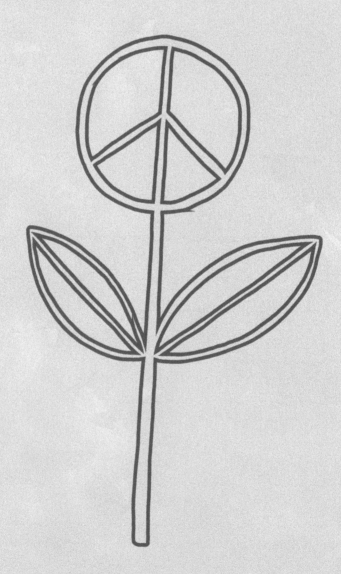

Respond, DON'T React

While self-love encourages you to feel your feelings, some emotions can be overwhelming. When strong emotions flood you, you are likely to **react** immediately. A reaction is impulsive and is usually guided by your own negative self-beliefs. **Responding**, however, is respecting and understanding how you feel—then, with logic and context, purposefully deciding how to navigate the situation. You respect your feelings and what they are trying to communicate to you, but emotion is not in the driver's seat. This exercise encourages you to build in a **pause** between a situation and your **response**. By giving yourself a pause, you can take time to consider why these feelings are strong within you, decide on the best way to meet your needs, then calmly and sensibly respond. Consider a situation that you anticipate may trigger big emotions in you, or use a situation from the past. In the pause space below, identify ways you can create space between the situation and your response. For example, ask for some time, don't respond to texts right away, remove yourself from the situation, take a deep breath and count to 10, etc.

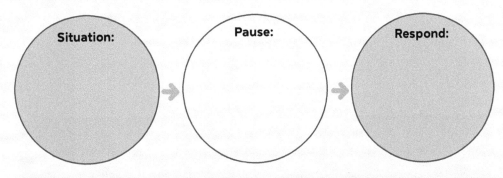

Situation: Pause: Respond:

TIPS & TRICKS: *Keyboard Expression*

On tough days when you need to vent quickly, try some free expression. Use a detached keyboard or a laptop keyboard with the computer turned off. Type out how you are feeling, knowing that the words are vanishing into thin air. You don't need to censor or worry about spelling or grammar. Once you have expressed yourself fully, take a deep breath in and out. The thoughts and feelings have made their way out of you. You can release yourself from their burden and return to yourself and your day.

Meaningful Music

Having a tough day? Jamming out may be the solution! Music is known to have positive psychological impacts. It can help release a chemical in the brain, known as dopamine, that helps you feel good. Music can inspire, reduce anxiety, and improve your mood. When a bad day sneaks up on you, having a playlist of songs may be helpful. Write a list of empowering songs that may inspire some self-love and get you through a rough time. Identify songs that remind you of your power, worth, love, and self-respect.

My Meaningful Music

- _____
- _____
- _____
- _____
- _____
- _____
- _____

- _____
- _____
- _____
- _____
- _____
- _____
- _____

SELF-LOVE IN ACTION: *Love Is in the Arts*

Artistic expression is an effective way to increase self-worth. When you need a boost, turn toward the arts. You do not have to be naturally artistic or have any skill. It's an opportunity for expression just as you are. Here are a few ideas: singing, playing a new instrument, drawing, painting, dancing, writing, poetry, creating a manga or comic, crafting, making jewelry, coloring, photography, film, decorating your room, fashion, makeup. There are endless options of artistic expression. Just enjoy the process of creation. Consider how you feel about yourself as you express yourself in this new way.

You're My People

Earlier in the book, you learned that it's okay to ask for help. You can turn to people for support, help, or just to distract you when you need a break. Thriving in life does not happen in isolation. One of the biggest acts of self-love is asking for support when you need it! In each box below, identify people who might be able to provide support. It's okay if the same person is in several boxes. Who can distract you? Who can you ask for help when you are struggling in school? Who helps provide you emotional support? These are your people.

DISTRACTION

EXTRACURRICULAR

OTHER

ACADEMIC

EMOTIONAL

The Takeaway

Think back on all the work you have done while using this book. If you even made one or two small changes to develop self-love, then you should be proud! In the spaces below, write down any lessons, insights, or changes you have made that you want to take away from this experience.

MY TAKEAWAYS

LEARNING TO LOVE

I will ride the waves of life knowing I am capable, lovable, supported, and strong.

Self-Love Assessment Quiz: The Retake

You made it to the final exercise! I know most quiz retakes are dreaded, but hopefully this one inspires you to keep building your self-love resources. Let's retake the self-love quiz from the very beginning of this workbook. See the progress you've made and what areas might benefit from more practice. Rate the following statements from 0 to 5, then total up your responses at the end.

0 = never   2 = sometimes   4 = most of the time

1 = rarely   3 = frequently   5 = always

1. I believe I am good enough and valuable.

0   1   2   3   4   5

2. It is okay for me to make mistakes and not be perfect.

0   1   2   3   4   5

3. I can communicate what I need and want with ease.

0   1   2   3   4   5

4. I know when I am struggling and know how to support myself in those times.

0   1   2   3   4   5

5. I believe I am worthy and deserving of love.

0   1   2   3   4   5

6. I accept and love my body just as it is.

0   1   2   3   4   5

7. I know my abilities and strengths and how to use them when I face challenges.

0   1   2   3   4   5

CONTINUED >>

8. My feelings are just as important as everyone else's.

   0   1   2   3   4   5

9. I do not need romantic relationships or validation from friends to feel good about myself.

   0   1   2   3   4   5

10. I make a point to take care of myself and do nice things for myself.

    0   1   2   3   4   5

SCORE:

40–50: Self-love rock star! You have a strong ability to love yourself. Keep going strong!

30–39: You have a strong foundation of self-love. Keep learning and practicing ways to strengthen your self-love abilities.

20–29: There are days you feel good about yourself and days you struggle. The more you invest in yourself with practice and patience, the more good days you will have. Don't stop!

10–19: Loving yourself fully is a challenge. But you are capable of learning how to value yourself. You're already on your way!

0–9: You're a self-love newbie. But you are capable, important, and ready to start. You're in the right place. Let's do this!

REFLECTION:

....

....

....

....

....

....

You Are Worth It

You made it to the end! I hope that engaging with this workbook has helped you remove some of the bricks of self-criticism and self-doubt from your backpack and that you are beginning to feel lighter and freer. While this book is a good start, it's not an immediate cure to the self-love problem. Just like with any new skill, you need practice, patience, and daily intention to see long-lasting change and growth. Hopefully, you have learned ways to keep working at self-love every day. Anytime you feel like you've veered off course, just pick the book back up and give your brain some reminders. If you take nothing else away from this experience, remember this: *You are import-ant. You are valuable. You matter.* Hold this wisdom close to your heart and acknowledge it every single day. Shine bright!

> "We just need to be kinder to ourselves.
> If we treated ourselves the way
> we treated our best friend, can you
> imagine how much better off we would be?"
>
> —MEGHAN MARKLE

RESOURCES FOR TEENS

Personality Test Links

Enneagram Personality Test: *EnneagramInstitute.com*
The Myers-Brigg Personality Test: *16Personalities.com*

Mood Monitoring Apps

Daylio

Moodnotes

Mood Ring

Moody

Reflectly

Meditation/Well-Being Apps

Aura

Be Okay

Breathe

Happify

Headspace

Meditation Oasis

Videos and TV

Headspace Guide to Meditation *(Netflix, 2021)*
  Netflix.com/title/81280926
Headspace Guide to Sleep *(Netflix, 2021)*
  Netflix.com/title/81328827
Headspace Unwind Your Mind *(Netflix, 2021)*
  Netflix.com/title/81328829
Helen Whitener—TEDx Talk, "Claiming Your Identity by Understanding
  Your Self-Worth"
  YouTu.be/57FMau29O_g
  YouTube Channel: MyLife
Kristin Neff—TEDx Talk, "The Space Between Self-Esteem and
  Self Compassion"
  YouTu.be/IvtZBUSplr4

Websites

The Body Image Movement
  BodyImageMovement.com
Information, books, documentary, and resources for body positivity.
  "What Is Self-Worth and How Do We Increase It?"
  PositivePsychology.com/self-worth

Books/Journals

The Girls' Guide to Growth Mindset: A Can-Do Approach to Building Confidence, Courage, and Grit by Kendra Coates

Mindfulness for Teens in 10 Minutes a Day: Exercises to Feel Calm, Stay Focused & Be Your Best Self by Jennie Marie Battistin

The Mindfulness Journal for Teens: Prompts and Practices to Help You Stay Cool, Calm, and Present by Jennie Marie Battistin

Self-Love Journal for Teen Girls: Prompts and Practices to Inspire Confidence and Celebrate You by Cindy Whitehead

Crisis and Immediate Support

Crisis Intervention for LGBTQ Youth: The Trevor Project – *1-866-488-7386 or Thetrevorproject.org*

National Eating Disorders Association – *NationalEatingDisorders.org*

National Domestic Violence Hotline – *1-800-799-SAFE (7233) or TheHotline.org*

National Sexual Abuse Hotline – *1-800-656-HOPE (4673) or RAINN.org*

National Suicide Prevention Hotline – *1-800-273-TALK (8255) or SuicidePreventionLifeline.org/help-yourself/youth*

RESOURCES FOR PARENTS

Books

Brainstorm: The Power and Purpose of the Teenage Brain by Daniel J. Siegel, MD

Love Her Well by Kari Kampakis

Mindfulness Journal for Parents: Prompts and Practices to Stay Calm, Present, and Connected by Josephine Atluri

Mindful Parenting in a Chaotic World: Effective Strategies to Stay Centered at Home and On-the-Go by Nicole Libin, PhD

Self-Love Workbook for Women: Release Self-Doubt, Build Self-Compassion, and Embrace Who You Are by Megan Logan

The Teenage Brain: A Neuroscientist's Survival Guide to Raising Adolescent and Young Adults by Frances Jensen, MD, with Amy Ellis Nutt

The Yes Brain: How to Cultivate Courage, Curiosity, and Resilience in Your Child by Daniel Siegel, MD, and Tina Payne Bryson, PhD

Untangled: Guiding Teenage Girls Through the Seven Transitions into Adulthood by Lisa Damour, PhD

Online

All Things Brené Brown
BreneBrown.com
Barb Steinberg, "An Easy Way to Boost Your Daughter's Self-Esteem"
YouTube.com/watch?v=T3obewRXbqY
Helen Whitener—TEDx Talk, "Claiming Your Identity by Understanding
Your Self-Worth"
YouTube.com/watch?v=57FMau29O_g
Kimber Lybertt—TEDx Talk, "Dear Grown-ups . . . Sincerely, Gen Z"
YouTube.com/watch?v=P0xIoUhzpvA
Kristin Neff—Self-Compassion
Self-Compassion.org
Kristin Neff—TEDX Talk, "The Space Between Self-Esteem and
Self Compassion"
YouTube.com/watch?v=IvtZBUSplr4&t=0s
"What Is Self-Worth and How Do We Increase It?"
PositivePsychology.com/self-worth

REFERENCES

Ackerman, Courtney E. "What Is Self-Worth and How Do We Increase It?" PositivePsychology.com/self-worth.

Chansard, Tabatha, PhD. *Conquer Anxiety Workbook for Teens: Find Peace from Worry, Panic, Fear, and Phobias*. Emeryville, CA: Althea Press, 2019.

Damour, Lisa, PhD. *Untangled: Guiding Teenage Girls Through the Seven Transitions into Adulthood*. New York, NY: Ballantine Books, 2017.

Gilmore, Karen J., MD, and Pamela Meersand, PhD. *Normal Child and Adolescent Development: A Psychodynamic Primer*. Arlington, VA: American Psychiatric Publishing, 2014.

Golemman, Daniel. *Emotional Intelligence: Why It Can Matter More than IQ*. New York, NY: Bantam Books, 1995.

Golemman, Daniel. *Social Intelligence: The New Science of Human Relationships*. New York, NY: Bantam Dell, 2006.

Harvard Business Review Emotional Intelligence Series. *Self-Awareness*. Boston, MA: Harvard Business Review Press, 2019.

Jensen, Frances E., MD, with Amy Ellis Nutt. *The Teenage Brain: A Neuroscientist's Survival Guide to Raising Adolescents and Young Adults*. New York, NY: HarperCollins, 2015.

Kabat-Zinn, Jon. *Wherever You Go There You Are: Mindfulness Meditation in Everyday Life*. New York, NY: Hyperion, 1994.

Logan, Megan. *Self-Love Workbook for Women: Release Self-Doubt, Build Self-Compassion, and Embrace Who You Are*. Emeryville, CA: Rockridge Press, 2020.

Neff, Kristin, PhD. *Self-Compassion: The Proven Power of Being Kind to Yourself.* New York, NY: HarperCollins, 2011.

Pour, Nafiseh H., Gholam Reza Mahmoodi-Shan, Abbas Ebadi, and Nasser Behnampour. "Spiritual Self-Care in Adolescents: A Qualitative Study." *International Journal of Adolescent Medicine and Health.* Pre-Published online by De Gruyter (October 16, 2020). DOI.org/10.1515/ijamh-2019-0248.

Siegel, Daniel J., MD. *Brainstorm: The Power and Purpose of the Teenage Brain.* New York, NY: TarcherPerigee, 2013.

INDEX

Acknowledgments

Words cannot express my gratitude to my patients, who have taught me as much as I have taught them. Their insights, strength, growth, and their own creative ideas for self-love are on every page of this book. They are inspiring in every way possible. They have contributed to my growth as a therapist and hopefully will inspire others to do this difficult and rewarding work, too!

To my family and friends, you, too, have helped me in my own journey of self-love and encouraged me to be a stronger, more confident, and self-compassionate human. Thank you for your unconditional support and love.

About the Author

 **Tabatha Chansard, PhD,** is a licensed clinical psychologist specializing in cognitive behavioral therapy for a variety of emotional and behavioral difficulties. Dr. Chansard received her doctoral degree in clinical psychology from the APA-accredited program at the University of Texas Southwestern Medical Center. During her training, she served as chief resident and worked with children, adolescents, and adults in a variety of clinical and medical settings.

Dr. Chansard currently operates a private practice and is passionate about her specialized work with children, adolescents, and young adults. She is the author of *Conquer Anxiety Workbook for Teens: Find Peace from Worry, Panic, Fear, and Phobias.* Her expertise has been featured in informational podcasts and health and wellness websites.